BE TRANSCENDENT

TO SUSTAIN

HAPPINESS

BE TRANSCENDENT TO SUSTAIN HAPPINESS
Ethics Philosophical Essays—Reduce Miseries and Stresses

ISBN: 979-8-9860364-0-3 (Print)
ISBN: 979-8-9860364-1-0 (eBook)

Library of Congress Control Number: 2022910918

Editing by Mark Meyer.

Cover design by Michelle Argyle.
Book design by Michelle Argyle.

Author photograph Rose Love Innocent Milien.

Printed by Ingram Spark

Published by yMilien
Baldwin, New York

Visit www.yvonmilien.com

ETHICS PHILOSOPHICAL ESSAYS

Reduce Miseries and Stresses

YVON MILIEN

Also by Yvon Milien

The Rhythm of My Life:
Tuning into the Rocky Rhythm of Fire

Author's Note

Wisdom is the leverage we need to find happiness in this world. We are born to develop and practice wisdom to understand ourselves, be tolerant, support each other, and not be like malicious wild animals.

However, wisdom cannot be developed and practiced if we ignore the concept of morals, laws, will, the mind, and imagination. And without understanding, we cannot be happy. These are concepts that consistently give rise to disagreements, especially nowadays. People who may disagree with the focus of these concepts in this book may be offended. I had no intention to insult anybody. If some people are offended, I frankly apologize. These concepts are like bedsheets. When it is cold, and we share a bed with others, in our case, considering that life is the bed, we will always try to pull them on our side to cover ourselves. It is a natural human attitude, and such an attitude will never change. So, controversies around these concepts are forever or till the end of this world if it will end indeed.

Thus, if I pull the sheet too much on my side to shield myself, I am sorry. Please forgive me; it is because my practice works for me. In this cold world, I feel warm and secure under my understanding. That is why I am still happily alive and keep going on with my life. Every day I strive to develop and practice the ideas developed in this book in my life. If this kind of understanding works for me, it may work for many of you, that is to say, maintaining happiness.

Life is very complex, making happiness merely an affair of genuine intelligence, not continued follies. This book is not a shortcut to make the pursuit of happiness an easy task, but to help develop an understanding and the courage to fight for joy. I hope this book can inspire readers to strive for inner happiness by controlling their actions with the heavenly tools that God blesses them with and enjoy their lives under fewer stresses.

If we are not prepared to fulfill our life to live happily, we will never experience joy and inspire others to achieve a sense of their true self and purpose to live happily. Without preparation to be happy, we will only have some flashes of the cheap, exciting moments when we satisfy our lower self. Afterward, like gravity pulls things down to the surface of the earth, our unfulfilling life will always pull us down to reality. And regrettably, we will spend our lives chasing happiness like people pursuing their shadow.

I hope this book fulfills its purpose of teaching something valuable about life, contributing to self-realization, increasing readers' inner light and decreasing darkness, and fending off life problems trying to steal happiness.

Considering nowadays few people are interested in self-convincing themselves to reduce their miseries, and stresses, I asked myself, will writing this book be worthy of consideration? I am writing this book to persuade myself to continue to be transcendent to sustain happiness. I believe that authors should write to convince themselves first while speaking about wholesome topics and let the consequences follow, that is to say, if some people think that what they read is helpful to them, okay! For those who believe otherwise, that is okay too! Everybody is free to live their own life, after all. Whether political, social, economic, or mainly administrative, leaders can put this thinking into practice.

Since self-realization is a full-time job, every action we do or take should be a step toward our self-development. To sustain our happiness, we must realize ourselves. Therefore, maintaining happiness is also a full-time job.

The being (nature) of the Good is a certain Will;
the being of the Bad is a certain kind of Will.
What then are externals? Materials for the Will, about
which the will being conversant shall obtain its own good
or evil. How shall it obtain the good. If it does not admire
(overvalue) the materials; for the opinions about the
materials, if the opinions are right, make the will good: but
perverse and distorted opinions make the will bad.

Epictetus, Discourses, Book I, XXIX

Contents

Chapter 1

Strive Not to Put the Plow Before the Oxen

A proverb says, "to put the plow in front (or before) of the oxen," which means starting with where we should end, which is not a good strategy for moving forward. When we are focused first on satisfying our material desires, not our self-development, doesn't it look like we are putting our plow in front of our oxen? Then, if this is the case, can we see that our life is not progressing, and there is no way we can be happy? So, it would be best to do the right action, start with where we should begin—with our self-development.

We may understand this proverb, and it may make perfect sense to us, but we may continue to put the plow before the oxen because we are not aware that we are not moving forward; therefore, we just let our life stay stagnant. But, if we want to move forward with our life, we need to change our strategy, and such change may be difficult for us to do with our current lifestyle. Thus, we may believe that it is impossible to direct our conduct in social, political, economic, and spiritual life by proverbs. Well, listen to Schopenhauer (1957), who said, "[We] must not believe, that it is impossible to direct our conduct in social life by rules, maxims and that it is better, therefore, just to let ourselves go. [The key is] with this as with all practical instructions: understanding the rule is one thing; learning to apply it is another. The first is acquired at once by intelligence; the second is gradually developed through exercise." So, once we develop the understanding, pull ourselves together, and practice, then when we practice good maxims, we will be happy, and we will work to make others comfortable around us. Unconsciously, our presence will make others feel good even though they may not like us.

Imagine a nation where seventy-five percent of its population is self-developed and has self-control. This move would be equivalent to seventy-five percent of citizens being vaccinated for Covid-19 to immunize themselves against the virus to protect themselves and others. The seventy-five percent of the self-developed population would create a safer environment for that nation because most minds would be protected against the toxic mentality that makes each other miserable due to greed, lust, anger, hate, and dishonesty. Most people of the population would feel safe and be happy in this world. In the same way that the leaders do their best to focus on a vaccine to stop Covid-19, why can't they do the same to focus on coming up with the best education system to help people develop themselves? Why don't they make it easy for kids and adolescents in their schools to be exposed to self-development knowledge? If they did, it could lead people to have a happy state of mind and a less fragmented nation. Why do educators not teach students that the purpose of life is not to strive to live longer in this world and to enjoy material goods, but to have a productive inner life and get ready to move back where they come from, the source?

Some people may argue that because it would cripple every capitalist economy. On the other hand, others may object that a capitalist economy with considerable self-developed employees would generate more profit because its workers will be more productive and eager to support capitalism for collective goals and well-being. A case in point is Japan's economy. The article by Yamamoto and Lloyd (2019), "Ethical Considerations of Japanese Business Culture," tells us how the culture of self-realization affects the Japanese business culture. According to the article, Japan's economic progress connects to two spiritual dimensions: the normative spiritual of individuals, and group and collective. In the first spiritual context, each individual is considered to have a spiritual element or life force within. Confucianism, Buddhism, and Shintoism have supported this belief. In the second spiritual normative, a group or society has its universal life force. The first spiritual dimension entails norms of personal development behavior in relation to the universe, while the second encourages group support. Thus, according to Taka (see Yamamoto et al., 2019), individuals help each other and encourage each other to reach their potential, leading to the spiritual development of both individuals and the group.

Japanese transcendental principles orient them to their personal development to benefit society. The immaterial normative ethics culture is shared in the Japanese business environment. As a result, citizens see work as holy and honorable. Moreover, employees develop loyalty to their employers, peers, and the system and leaders show enough fairness in return to them.

So, the Japanese unique traditional business ethics culture has made Japan's economy thriving so far. However, unfortunately, sound principles have unintended consequences. It is

3

not uncommon for some people in a given society to interpret, understand, and experience a good system in rather radical ways. So, some Japanese develop a work-centric attitude. As a result, they are working long and hard, and their health deteriorates, both mentally and physically, and they commit suicide from constantly working overtime. As the Bhagavad-Gita suggested, we should regulate our habits, discipline our mental activities to become situated in transcendence.

Any politician, administrator, and educator whose plan is to focus on the prosperity of a state without considering first the self-development of the citizen, is putting the plow before the oxen. Their unawareness leads them to start with where they should have ended.

It is common sense that we will never abide by the regulations if we do not have self-control. It is not the laws that make people obey the rules, whether divine, natural, or governmental, but merely self-development and self-control. If we cannot control ourselves, we will never be able to obey any law or keep a vow, we will always get into trouble and we will never be happy. Anybody who has the slightest amount of common sense will understand that.

Again, when we put the law before self-control and self-development, we set the plow before the oxen. Therefore, the result will be chaotic, and we will fail miserably. There is no incredible magic in this world other than self-development and self-control. Such an attitude proves that we love ourselves and others and are ready to support the collective goals and well-being. Our interest in personal growth and restraint demonstrates that we have the proper will and the right knowledge.

Goodwill and proper knowledge are the fundamental pillars of happiness. Material possessions and earthly powers such as political, economic, and social influence are like smoke pillars, and they cannot sustain happiness in and of themselves; history testifies to that. Observe the lives of some wealthy people, politicians, and the famous, and see how they treat each other and act. It seems that these people merely have a boring rich life.

One of the keys to fulfillment without compromising the chance of other people to realize their happiness is to develop good intentions and sound practices. As soon as we understand the importance of developing good resolution and know what to want, we reinforce our "free will" and have the power to exercise a direct action on the ordinary events of life.

Understand that we cannot be happy if we do not know our composition well and make good choices to transcend our limitations and develop our immense abilities to grow. Transcendental knowledge and the will to learn how to act correctly are sure ways to sustain happiness in this life.

Self-transformation requires we develop strong beliefs that we are a soul, an entity whose task in this world is to evolve by experience. We are a vehicle of the divine spirit, the invisible and immortal principle within us, our divine essence, the spark of the Great Light within us, which is not extinguishable, not a body that must satisfy its craving at the expense of others. We must understand that our physical death is not the end of our life because our soul or individuality, the discrete, animate, personalized being, cannot die because it is not composed of cells or atoms. However, depending on our inclinations, our soul may degenerate by our experiences, though it cannot be divided because it is immeasurable and invisible. When we voluntarily make our soul the vessel of the divine spirit, it becomes invulnerable, a sacred part in us. When we believe that our blessed soul, our divine individuality, is our undeniable property, and that no force in the world can squash it or deprive us of it, we become a spiritual being.

5

We must not be concerned with our body, instincts, deductive intelligence, race, ethnic background, gender, size, height—in a word, with our personality, the fleeting. Our personality, the lower ego, disappears with the destruction of our body. History and others are more likely only to remember our acts than the body. When we spend our lives caring only for our body and our more subordinate individuality, we are betting on the capricious, meaning that we live in vain. And how can somebody who lives in smug sustain happiness? How can someone bet on the precarious, who only wants to satisfy the lower ego, be content? It will be challenging to be delighted during our lives if we do not commit to helping others but only to our inferior egos. We need to focus on the invisible power behind what we see and believe in providence and our divine birthright. Again, when we give more importance to the lower personality, the body, we put the plow in front (or before) of the oxen.

We should not develop an inordinate affection for the material world in order to not be concerned for the satisfaction of our senses. Our eyes are like windows in our house, and if we keep constantly looking through them, we will never accomplish our self-realization because we will be distracted by so many insignificant things.

Nevertheless! We have the freedom to be whatever we believe we should be, care for whatever we think we should, put the plow before the oxen, but sooner or later, the consequences will follow. So, life will prove if we are on the right or the wrong path. And make no mistake, we will have our reward at the end of the day!

But know that our fate is to upgrade, not to degrade ourselves and others. We should be willing to be led by our destiny, and we should never make it a priority to please others and our lower self. One of our dearest desires should be to open other eyes and keep our eyes open in upgrading others as well as us so that we can please God, the Almighty, our Creator.

If we are reluctant to be led by our destiny, we are willing to please others and our lower ego. And our fate will be dragged by life. It does not make sense to dedicate our life to satisfying the caprices of others and our lower ego because others and our lower self are ephemeral, sometimes deceptive, and ungracious. So, they cannot sustain our happiness.

Chapter 2

Have a Story, Not a History

"The story of an [individual] is the story of his/[her] feeling of inferiority [weakness] and his/[her] attempts to resolve it," said Emmanuel Mounier (1974). We cannot have a story if we do not strive to remedy our weaknesses to inspire others to improve themselves and give happiness. Then, we will have a history of acting irresponsibly. Likewise, civilizations, nations, and institutions will have histories but no stories to tell when they focus on fructifying, glamorizing their greed, injustices, lust, and making wars. They will have a record of greed, injustices, causing wars, crimes, prostitution, and destruction. We make history by conquering and controlling others, but we make a story by dominating and managing ourselves.

In this context, spiritually speaking, our histories are a series of events connected with our weaknesses; at the same time, our stories are the account of events in the evolution of our life that could inspire others to aim at their progression to strive for peace and happiness. Of course, when our primary motive is to satisfy our lower ego and we are willing to destroy people and our country, we will make history for sure, and the media will talk about it before and after our death. However, if everything we do in our life is to make a positive difference in this world, we are creating a story, and the mundane media are more likely not to talk about us while we are alive, and maybe even when we are no longer in this world. Case in point, the mundane media do not very often talk about inspiring stories or good books, but we will see a lot of nonsense celebrities' histories that could never improve our life, covered every day.

We are born with weaknesses and strengths. From the day we were born to adolescence, our parents, institutions, government, and environments must guide us in our development. From young adult to our exit in this world, we must have an inspiring story about our life. Otherwise, we will never have peace, and how can we sustain our happiness in this world if we cannot have peace? So, the Bhagavad-Gita is correct: no peace, no joy.

To succeed in our attempts to resolve our weaknesses, we must first find out what type of weaknesses we have and acknowledge that we have them; be honest with ourselves. Then, emphasize in our mind the main disadvantages of our shortcomings and the advantages of getting rid of them to encourage us not to get carried away by them and to take the necessary steps to find a solution.

If we do not have an inspiring story about our life, a story that shows that as a human being, we have the courage and the stamina to overcome our weaknesses, we have lived in vain. Our account can be as simple as overcoming a simple flaw, for instance, being unfaithful to our spouse, which is a weakness because it can grow into a much larger problem; we or our spouse, or the other leg of the love triangle, may get killed.

With the help of transcendental knowledge, we can overcome any weakness, but we have to develop the will. Besides, our parents, institutions, government, spiritual leaders, environment, and good books need to inspire us and guide us to acquire such knowledge and develop the will. This task should not be temporary; instead, it should be a constant one. Unfortunately, some of us may be placed in an unfavorable environment that could not inspire, guide us, or improve our knowledge to overcome our weaknesses. However, we can still look for the opportunity to learn how to overcome them later. Better late than never creating our story. As a result, we will have a more exciting account in such a case.

We may have one or a thousand weaknesses; to overcome them and have peace and sustain happiness, we need to understand ourselves first. We need to know who we are. We need to know the laws that govern us and learn how to observe them and strive to abide by them to live in peace in our mind, to have fewer regrets at the end of the day. Indeed, such an endeavor is not a simple or easy task, but it is worthwhile to try it.

It is okay to have weaknesses, but it is not okay to grow them like growing fruits to eat healthily—that is not healthy for our mind or our soul. Drawbacks will not help us in our evolution. We need to beware that weakness can take many forms; it can be so subtle that we can believe it is a strength, and others will take advantage of us by encouraging us to grow such softness. For instance, if we have a naive perception that helping others means letting them use us for their benefits, it is a weakness because it is a distorted perception about assisting others that leaves us open to abuse. Furthermore, such an attitude means that we do not understand the material world. We are not more vital when we let others take advantage of us and not confront them. Instead, we are weakening our psychic or mental powers. We need to exercise this power to grow it and to be happy. We may feel very weak after we let someone shamefully use us, and this is because our psychic power diminished, while the person who cons us may feel more vigorous. Therefore to sustain our happiness, we need to protect ourselves from getting scammed by others, and when they succeed on one occasion, we need to stop them.

Making history is easy because it does not require knowledge, wisdom, goodwill, or truthfulness. All it needs is the nerve, audacity, appropriate means, gang backup, and ignorance to carry out despicable actions. With such an approach, we will make history for sure. While creating a story is a different ball game because it requires a lot of knowledge about life, especially ourselves, great wisdom, goodwill, and truthfulness, this approach takes time, courage, and the patience to develop acceptance of unpopularity. Creating our story instead of our history has a significant advantage in that we can live through our story and revisit it very often to refresh our happiness. We cannot do the same with our history because our history has the potential to bury us like a dead person and degrade our soul.

We will sustain our happiness and create a story when we believe we are a Spiritual Being and understand that spirituality is KNOWING before experiencing the divine experience. If we want to experience the divine experience to create an inspiring story, we must understand it. The only way to understand the divine experience is to develop knowledge about it, understand the laws and principles that govern it, and know ourselves. And we must convince and persuade ourselves that the proper knowledge will lead us to that end.

Note that we cannot experience what we do not understand. It is crucial to realize that we can only feel what we know, and we will better understand in the long run, that is, internalize what we have experienced. For instance, happiness, health, fear, and love are concrete nouns for things we will not see because they do not physically exist, but we may trust or believe them to exist. We can for sure know that these abstract nouns exist when we experience them. So, it is true that we will understand happiness, health, fear, and love better when we feel them. So, to sustain our happiness, we must strive to understand the meaning of the concept of happiness.

We must understand health, fear, and love, meaning that we must experience them to enjoy happiness. For instance, if we are healthy and have a loving heart, we will be automatically happy. According to Herophilus (1989), "[W]hen health is absent, wisdom cannot reveal itself, art cannot manifest, strength cannot fight, wealth becomes useless, and intelligence cannot be applied;" therefore, we cannot sustain happiness. Our health may depend on external factors, but we have the power to adapt and survive in a hostile environment. Any external thing is always under internal control when we develop the proper will and knowledge. A simple way to shut down the toxic external factor, to paraphrase the former professional heavyweight boxer Ed Latimore (2017), is to be busy building our own life, taking care of our health, that other people's bullshit (especially the so-called celebrities) is of no concern to us. To achieve this goal, we need to be tolerant with others or love them no matter what, and we need to be strict with ourselves, as Marcus Aurelius suggested in his *Meditations*. When we develop a forgiving, loving mind free from other people's bullshit, we will know how to care for ourselves and others. To paraphrase Lao Tzu (Chapter 50), we will not need to shun the rhinoceros or the tiger, we need not fear weapons even in the midst of the battle of life. The rhinoceros finds no place into which to thrust its horn; the tiger no place into which to fix its claws; nor the sword a place into which to flesh its point. We will have time to develop ourselves to move from the mortal to the immortal state of mind and obtain enlightenment because we kill that desire to be concerned about other people's bullshit and be tolerant of living healthy.

On the other hand, when we experience fear, we will know that happiness is a sweet feeling that is different from fear, and we will understand that we should avoid putting loved ones in a fearful situation.

How do we prove that we understand something? We can prove that we "understand" something if we can explain, infer, relate, and assess. For example, consider "happiness." First, we need to be able to demonstrate that it is a state of well-being and contentment. This state relates to many key factors, such as divine knowledge, self-knowledge, self-development, purpose in life, and abiding by the laws, whether they are holy, moral, or governmental. We can infer that our heart cannot swell with happiness if we do not develop such knowledge and control ourselves. Last but not least, we need to assess how much we know to continue to improve our ability to create ourselves and sustain our happiness. Once we acquire this understanding, we need to convince and persuade ourselves that we get it.

Chapter 3

Convincing and Persuading

When we are convinced and persuaded that a particular path is the best track to follow, we will be more likely to go in that direction without hesitation, no matter what people say, even if the course is dangerous and will lead to our perils.

According to Schuré (1960), the purpose of the ancient Egyptian temples was to develop great souls and servants for the progress of humankind. Opposite to Babylon, the dark metropolis of despotism, Egypt was in the ancient world a veritable citadel of sacred science, a school for its most illustrious prophets, a refuge and a laboratory of the noblest traditions of humanity. The esoteric doctrines of the priests of Egypt were cultivated in the temples, carefully veiled under the mysteries.

Hermes-Thoth is the first, the great initiator of Egypt to the sacred doctrines, undoubtedly relates to a first and peaceful mixture of the white race and the black race, in the regions of Ethiopia and upper Egypt, according to Schuré. The Greeks, disciples of the Egyptians, called him Hermes Trismegistus or "three times great" because he was considered king, legislator, and priest. He typified when the priesthood, the magistracy, and royalty were united in a single governing body. The Romans called him Mercury.

The Egyptians attributed forty-two books written on stones on occult science to Hermes. The Greek book known as *Hermes Trismegistus* contains certainly altered content. But, still, infinitely precious remnants of the ancient theogony, which is known as *fiat lux*. And from which many great initiates in that era received their first rays. The doctrine of Fire-Principle and the Word-Light contained in the *Vision of Hermes* was the climax and center of Egyptian initiation in the development of great souls and servants for the progress of humanity.

Throughout the ages, the great philosophers, artists, and saints have worked in that direction to help humanity moving forward. The religious institutions and philosophers used the art of convincing and persuading simultaneously to help humankind welcome the truth. The ancient sages understood that if a teacher or a guide failed to support an adherent to develop a firm conviction, which is the adherence or assent of the intelligence to the absolute truth, the pupil would never accept the fact. Conviction deals with the mind, so the disciple needs to be convinced about reality.

Furthermore, if a teacher or guide does not focus on persuading, which is the adhesion or consent of the heart to accept the truth, the pupil would never feel it. When we feel the truth, it gets into our conscious who gives the subconscious order to accept it; then it becomes a reality for us because, as Goddard (1944) said, "Consciousness is the one and only reality." Persuasion deals mainly with the heart. For instance, it would be challenging for someone to believe that God exists, internalize a moral concept, a fact, if that someone does not feel it. People

15

believe or internalize what they feel. Being convinced implies an effort, a struggle to accept an idea. If people have any interest other than the truth, it will be challenging to convince them, even if someone demonstrates the fact. The bias motives of people will prevent them from accepting the truth. One must want to know the truth with the sound mind to be convinced and love the truth with the whole heart to be persuaded. Once this process is successful, the individual internalizes the truth.

Convincing and persuading are two different concepts. Our mind can consent to an idea, and we can give our permission to an opinion without being persuaded. Most of us are familiar with what preachers always warn us against: "We must not accept the gospel with our mind only," which means don't be convinced only. Our will must have consented to the truth.

But we can be persuaded without being convinced. For example, a teacher may lead us to believe by passion more than by evidence. Although, in this case, we may be a fanatic, our passionate attitude may become dangerous if carried out to the extreme. To paraphrase Blaise Pascal (Pensées, 282), a French mathematician, physicist, inventor, and writer, the only way for us to know the truth is through our reason and our heart.

Every day we are engaging in convincing and persuading ourselves at one level or another. We may prompt and entice ourselves to do or not to do something. The strategy used is the same for both doing or not doing something. We are maybe aware or unaware of that, but the fact is that we are using our mind and our heart to take our everyday actions, meaning that we have to convince and persuade ourselves first. For instance, to commit adultery or satisfy lust or a greedy action, to name these common vices, we have to use our brain to rationalize these vicious acts and make our heart feel these actions to make it excited. We see a beautiful or handsome person, and we want to have sex with that person. We have to demonstrate for our mind how great such a conquest will be for it and make our heart feel excited before the pleasure and bliss it may enjoy later while bragging about the escapade. We may know very well that our heart may not enjoy the sexual act in the moment because it was not there due to the immorality of the action, but boasting later may excite us, so we have to persuade our heart.

Similarly, to convince and persuade ourselves that being greedy is the best value for us, the simple action to get wealthy, we will rationalize the advantages of greed and then make our heart feel the benefits of embezzling money, the mansions, the powers, and the travels. It is hard for the ignorant to see the consequences of vices when they use all of their energies to convince and persuade themselves that they are regular activities. If we are intelligent, we would know that we are wasting a lot of energy that we could have used to develop ourselves. Note that the suggestions from this world to satisfy such vices will be in our face every second of every minute of every day. If we cannot resist them, we are doomed. There are so many physically beautiful or handsome people in this world and so much money we might want to have that we will have to dedicate our entire life to satisfying our lust and greed. It will help if we use our convincing and persuading skills for the one truth. We come into this transitory world to develop ourselves so that we can return to the source, not waste our life trying to convince and persuade ourselves to satisfy a myriad of selfish desires. The most foolish thing some people can do is waste time writing books to convince and persuade themselves and others that practicing a vice is good for them despite the visible deterioration of their bodies, minds, and souls.

It would be best to remember that it is vital to convince

17

and persuade ourselves that the divine truth is not a myth in our quest for self-development and happiness. In other words, we can only be happy when we know and accept the ultimate truth. When we are convinced and persuaded about the ultimate reality, we can experience the Divine, the Higher Self, as the Object or body of God. According to Kant's view (1975), Self and Object are not independent entities but reciprocal elements into the experience. If we start from Object, we are led to Self; we are directed to Object if we begin with Self. The experience of either one involves the knowledge of the other, and both depend on the prior occurrence of a certain synthetic proposition. For instance, if we fix our mind in God, we will be happy because we will be free from bondage, anger, lust, and greed. As a result, God will be pleased because the Almighty is satisfied with our state of mind.

Beginning from God, everything leads to us; and starting with us, everything leads to God. The experience of the Higher Self, God, involves our experience and vice versa. Remember that both Higher Self and us depend on the prior occurrence of a certain proposition whose truth value is determined by observation, which is synthetical. How could we experience the Higher Self on the preceding occurrence? If we worship, surrender ourselves to the Higher Self, or make the Object of our love the Higher Self, we may personify it. Accordingly, we may experience it. And reciprocally, the Higher Self will experience ourselves too because our happiness is his joy.

Besides, anything else we may worship or profess our love for, such as the body or material world, we will personify it and always be in communion with it. Vice versa, we will have that knowledge with us. Therefore, it is possible to partake in the attributes of God, whose purpose is to allow us to experience happiness with our understanding.

According to NASA scientists, our Galaxy, the Milky Way, is highly active because of ongoing construction projects to expand itself. First, we have old stars dying and being torn down, and then new ones are built. As Hermes Trismegistus states in *The Emerald Tablet*, "as above so below." We need ongoing construction, so we should be highly active like the universe. We have to tear down bad habits and thoughts to build up better ones to develop ourselves. And we must tirelessly strive to convince and persuade ourselves that our task is to build ourselves and motivate others to do the same to sustain happiness in this world.

Chapter 4

Only Proper Knowledge Will Help Find
Meaning in this Life

Consciousness is the ability to experience internal and external existence. Some people are not interested in the development of the inner existence part of consciousness. Therefore, they are less likely to see meaning in their lives even though they have large material possessions. They always want more and more materials, believing that more money and worldly possessions will give sense to their lives. So, in their bored state of mind, most of them look for purpose in pleasures, refusing to learn that a balance between the internal and the external existence is necessary. But unfortunately, these people inspire many of us to give more importance to material consciousness because of their apparent successes. And some of us take them for idols, and dream to live like them.

When the material consciousness is too dominant in us, we may develop greed, lust, and anger, which may inspire us to act unjustly and make life seem absurd. Consciously or unconsciously, based on our irrational actions, those who hate injustice and lack inner knowledge may see the universe as irrational, purposeless, meaningless, or chaotic. Therefore, for them, life, society, and the world are messy and have no meaning because God does not prompt intervention to stop the injustice. Hence, if we do not have inner strength and wisdom, we will give absurdism, especially the philosopher Camus (1942), reason, whose writing is spreading that the world is devoid of God and eternity. So our search for meaning, unity, and clarity is futile.

Life, indeed, has significant meaning, but it is our morbid desires married with ignorance that cloud its purpose in our mind. When we let the clouds station permanently in our mind, we will abandon life, which had no intention to leave us, and as a result, our existence will be absurd. This world is everything but absurd. This world is incendiary; it is prone to controversy because of moral, social, political, and economic issues and the perpetuation of ignorance.

When using a spiritual lens, we will see that the chaos is not in the universe or the world, but in our mind. Only a lack of vision will make us think God is a God of confusion. Let's paraphrase the lotus pond story that Medhurst (1975) uses in his translation with commentary of *The Tao-Teh-King: Sayings of Lao Tzu* to try to illustrate our lack of vision if we agree with Camus. Picture the world like a giant lotus pond, covered with broad green leaves and brilliant blooms that irresistibly attracts us like children. But, instead of content to admire, content to enjoy, without desiring to possess, we all wade into the water, sink in the slime, and desperately struggle for the fragile petals. So, in our petty struggle to own the green leaves, brilliant blooms, and flowers in the mud, instead of possessing what we covet, we are destroying them. Consequently, we develop the belief that everything in the pond was meaningless. We did not have the vision to see that we could have owned the flowers, every brilliant thing which irresistibly attracted us in the pond for good, if we did not desire to grab the slimy pond and that we are feeblest when we are grasping.

From ignorance, all of us create a human condition that makes it difficult to sustain happiness. We can only find meaning in this world through proper knowledge, science that gives perception of things visible and invisible. Proper knowledge is the right immunization our mind needs to fight meaninglessness. We need to inoculate our mind with genuine knowledge to find happiness. The precondition for happiness is knowledge of our composition, the principles of the divine, intellectual, physical, and personal world, and the spirit of the laws and virtues.

It is not so hard to avoid troubles and live happily. We can use our vision to determine whether or not taking a course of action is worthy of consideration. It is essential to have the proper knowledge to ride toward our self-realization and the correct knowing before experiencing our authentic self—that faculty to envision, to picture whether is it worthy of putting ourselves or others through a bad situation. Our vision must be clear, free from anger, lust, and greed to succeed in such an endeavor.

To sustain our happiness in a crisis, especially if the problem is connected to some psychological factors, to paraphrase Viktor Frankl (1988), we should strive to orient ourselves to the meaning or the purpose of our existence. In other terms, we should dare to develop the necessary knowledge to convince and persuade ourselves to give sense to our lives no matter the circumstances. A prerequisite is to understand the laws that govern us, especially the working of the law that connects the material being to the spiritual being. The link between the material and spiritual being in us is our intellect. And the mind partakes of both the material and the immaterial qualities. Therefore, we need to develop the intellectual side of our nature to facilitate a harmonious connection between the two. In addition, we need to strengthen our will to concentrate all power of our being on having productive desires.

We have to search for meaning in this material world to become one with God to develop our consciousness. If there is no meaning or purpose in our lives, God will cease to exist in our lives. Therefore, our minds' orientation to the positive intention is the first step to attaining spiritual happiness.

We are not going to internalize such knowledge overnight. On the contrary, it is a long process that requires determination, vision, and a genuine intellect that has the power to convince and persuade ourselves about the necessity of spiritual understanding. Indeed, in this brutal material world that constantly suggests that there is no divine world, that what we see, is what exists, we need a lot of wisdom to survive.

Chapter 5

A Glance About What is Happiness

According to Aristotle (2011), happiness is the end goal of life because it is the only thing needed to make the best of life, and also, it is "unconditionally complete." The first move we need to make to experience happiness is learning to discriminate between happiness and pleasure. Afterward, we find happiness in the spiritual realm and pleasure in the mundane sphere. The former is simple and easy to create, while the latter requires a mind craving for complex excitement to be manifested.

Happiness and pleasure require different approaches. One of the best approaches to happiness is high moral standards. When we are inclined to be virtuous, we can experience inner satisfaction. That inner satisfaction is the positive state of mind cultivated, influencing how happy we can be. On the other hand, the unethical approach makes us experience fleeting sensations brought on by something external. Pleasure is the various mental experiences we see as good, enjoyable, or worthwhile, independent of moral standards. Although fun pushes us to replicate satisfying events and circumstances, this lovely feeling is temporary, and most pleasure may carry disaster and regret after the fun experience. For instance, breaking a relationship to satisfy lust can be devastating for our family. In contrast, happiness has a long life span. Happiness is spiritual, and we can feel it as a sense of peace and satisfaction. At the same time, pleasure is instinctual, emotional, or animal. Therefore, it is possible to sense it when drinking or high.

Happiness is rational; while pleasure can be rational or irrational, it depends on our inclinations. We are human, so we need happiness and pleasure to cross the ocean of life. The former is divine, and the latter is human. Happiness is an inner experience related to internal harmony and psychological and emotional serenity. In contrast, pleasure is associated with physical feelings. However, pleasure is sound when good moral values guide it; if the satisfaction is for the sake of the primary part, our soul, it is reasonable. But, on the other hand, it is irrational when immoral values guide it and when it brings no contribution to make our soul feel delighted.

We may have fun in a relationship and not necessarily be happy. In this case, we will always be looking for new pleasures with other partners because the essential ingredient, love, is not there. By contrast, we may experience happiness and do not have fun. This situation happens when we work hard to achieve something and feel celestial joy. And each time we think about our success or others congratulate us, that feeling comes back. Also, we may find happiness in taking care of disabled loved ones when we take it to the level of doing our duties.

If we are not enlightened and we abide too long in a condition of happiness, it's easy to get tired of being happy and go for the experience of pleasures. Later we may express regret when we understand that pleasure is subordinated to happiness, and people who trade happiness for fun may have difficulty experiencing inner contentment again.

However, to be happy does not mean we have to be in an environment free of troubles, a perfect world. After all, God did not create this world to be heaven but a testing ground for humankind. That is why it is a temporary world. So, we have to learn to live with pain and pleasure and find inner happiness.

God made this world precisely the way it is, a battlefield for every living thing, including the trees and animals—survival of the fittest, survival of those who can think right for humankind's evolution. Unfortunately, many people in a position of power make survival something very close to the savage animals living in a jungle because they focus on sophisticated weaponry to intimidate, kill to survive, and find happiness.

Anyway, as soon as we leave the stage of infancy, our lives depend on thinking and logic. We will not survive and live happily in this world if we cannot use our minds to think courageously, protect ourselves, act right, and face hardship. To be happy, we have to endure good and bad times like the trees are always patiently enduring lousy weather and good weather. We need to develop virtues to be equally balanced between pleasure and pain. And, to paraphrase Pascal (Pensées, 352), the strength of the virtues developed must not be measured by our efforts but by our ordinary lives. According to Confucius (see Medhurst, 1975), "[t]hose who are without virtue, cannot abide long either in a condition of poverty and hardship or in a condition of enjoyment." Like good times, the disappointment of life is part of the package of being alive; we cannot subtract it from the equation. Expect that no matter how much effort we display, sometimes we will not obtain what we want so desperately. In Mencius (2004, see also Medhurst, 1975) terms, when our passion is disappointed, we should not stop practicing our principles for our good and the good of others so that we can sustain happiness. To maintain our contentment when things are not working our way, quoting a poem from Ugo Bassi (1885), we should:

"Measure [our] love by loss instead of gain;
Not by the wine drunk, but by the wine poured forth,
For love's strength [standout] in love's sacrifice,
And whoso suffers most [has] most to give."

The last line is not suitable for everyone. When the ignorant, the faint of heart, the wicked experience suffering, their negativities may explode to a point that they become highly vicious or dangerous. So, we should be the spiritually knowledgeable ones to maintain our humanity no matter what.

We may desire to have faithful families, friends, and no enemies, but the reality is that we will always have enemies no matter how pure our hearts are. Some people will always try to irritate us because they have a virus mentality. Like viruses whose mission is to infect other organisms and sometimes to destroy, to dominate, many people will always be ready to attack a healthy soul because that is their job to survive. These people take pleasure in irritating others for the sake of annoying us. Due to their ignorance, boredom, or having difficulty making sense of their life, some people who want to shine and lack the awareness to understand that they have the power to shine without exasperating others, commit evil. Possessed by a sick desire to destroy, they do not realize that they act like small, abject entities. They want to kill others to shine like a star. Because of their ignorance, they cannot see that the stars in the universe shine without destroying each other, but are merely radiating so that a soul could always enjoy their quiet, beautiful night show. This world exists to challenge our mind; we should constantly strive to make sense of our load of pretentious nonsense and maybe ourselves too, to find happiness.

Sound knowledge can help us make sense of life's difficulties. We should seek for knowledge that prompts us to be more concerned with the steadiness and direction of our thoughts than with trivial actions, which in the long run will inevitably degrade our mind and bring miseries upon us.

Develop knowledge that we can use to help others to have a better conception of life, and in this way to transform the evil in them into a good soul. We need to be bold and use the power of our positive spirit to be a model. To paraphrase Lao Tzu (Chapter 79), we should be ready to compromise hate and leave ill-will behind to sustain happiness. That is our battle for contentment. Therefore, the weapons of choice for our everyday life should not be the swords and lances of the Middle Ages, neither the modern weaponries. Instead, it should be our intuitive knowledge, a steady mind, a diamond soul to have the courage to be ourselves, to protect ourselves from the everyday nonsense of this world.

It is up to us to be happy or to develop happiness in our gut, in our soul. This task is within our power. We were made to evolve, not to regress, that is why we have laws; that is why we have Karma, karmic evolution. This world's purpose is to set the stage for the ultimate dual opportunity: happiness and suffering. According to Buddhism (see Thera, 1959), happiness comes from deliverance or detachment from the material world, and pain comes from bondage, greed, and lust. The chance to enter the stream of liberation or dominate the earth will always knock at our door. The opportunity to attain celestial joys or reign over the universe will always knock at our door. Still, it will be up to us to open our door to either deliverance or domination, to either celestial joys or reign over others. We should use our understanding to see which one is more important to our progression. To find happiness, we need to use our knowledge and apply moral laws to make sense of what seems not to make sense in our life. It is our right to look for happiness, but one of the ways to find true happiness is to work with natural, ethical, and legal laws. Therefore, we must know the function of rules, especially morals, which are more of an intelligent choice, a higher form of action to execute human affairs than legal laws. Adherence to morals may be challenging for us, so we need genuine educational training to develop our intelligence and reasoning faculty. What may make it so difficult for us to adhere to moral values is the freedom to act like the lowest creatures and the highest entities in the universe. For instance, we have the freedom to imitate viruses or stars, meaning that we have a limitless choice between the negative and the positive.

Happiness is a satisfying detached state of mind whether we are rich or poor, slim or fat, black or white, involved in a relationship or alone. It is a state of mind independent of material profit, loss, pain, sensual pleasure, weight, height, skin color, and gender. Still, it depends on our knowledge, ability to control ourselves, and integrity. A satisfied state of mind enjoys internal security, and it gives no importance to exterior protection. This state of mind can be manifested like a serene, beautiful, fresh morning feeling in the gut. It can be displayed like a lovely scented, relaxed evening in a tranquil park with a sky that looks like a masterpiece work of art lighted with the orange light of the setting sun enjoyment in the gut. It can be manifested like a sweet, satisfying feeling in the stomach when listening to our favorite melody.

Last but not least, happiness can be the marvelous feeling

in the gut when we fall in love. It would help if we always strived to sustain that delightful feeling in our mind. If we have time, we can go to a park and do some contemplation, or in a lovely corner of our house prepared for that; meditate, or try to remember the good times we spent with friends and family. We can also do something positive, like cook breakfast for our spouse or our children, do a good deed anyways to bring the good feeling to the stomach. We can put into practice the spiritual training we have; read a good book to help us sustain our happiness. This practice is to help us develop that habit of experiencing the good feelings in our gut. When we practice that habit and perfect it, it will become easy to surmount empty feelings in our soul when stressed.

As soon as we experience inner happiness, we must strive to make every day a sequel of the previous day in sustaining it. It would help if we believed that happiness results from self-worth, having a sense of dignity, and sound moral values, not what people think about us and how we look or our possessions. So, happiness comes from the tremendous inner drive, together with a well-informed purpose about life.

We should make it our duty to create the opportunity to experience this gut feeling. Please do not wait for others to make it happen. Instead, whether alone or in company with others, strive to create the opportunity and practice experiencing that feeling longer. And once we continue to practice, others will be surprised to see the natural glow of happiness on our faces, and they will be curious to find out what we did. And each time we tell interested people our secret, we should look in the mirror and be proud of ourselves because we inspired someone to be interested in genuine happiness.

It would be best not to count on hope to find happiness in some highly desperate situations but on resignation to find relief and be happy. Be honest to ourselves when we are experiencing a crisis that we have no power to stop. So, it would be best to display an attitude like Jesus by saying a simple prayer as He did on the Mount of Olives. Before his crucifixion, He prayed to God, asking Him to take away the cup, the suffering He would endure, from Him if He is willing. Jesus knew there was no way He could stop that execution, which is why He added in His prayer: "Yet not my will, but yours be done." He knew that, but hoping God might have changed His plan; stopping the execution would have been merely stretching His agony, not giving Him relief. But what should be done must be done, so the wisest thing He could do was to show His resignation, that is why he said, "not my will, but yours be done." That is the attitude we should always have when facing an intolerable situation that we have no power to fix to ease our sufferings. And if we endure to the end, we will be very soon glorified and enjoy the inner happiness when we survive the event. We know the story after His crucifixion, He was resurrected and sanctified by God and enjoyed eternal inner happiness. It indicates progress when we accept a situation with resignation if we cannot change it.

Happiness can flourish in any dire situation, like the most common types of cactus that live in the desert, if we are equipped with the divine will and have the proper knowledge. Happiness will not manifest and be sustained if we do not make an effort in that direction. Nothing good or bad will be displayed and maintained in this world if we are not determined to make it happen, if our will does not back it up.

If we lack courage, strength, and energy in our hearts to support our happiness, we will never be happy because happiness requires courage. Do what we have to do. Want what we must want. Do our duty, and be satisfied.

Only doing the right thing is beneficial, which means that we will never be happy when we get out of the right way. Therefore, it is a miscalculation to base happiness on means that righteousness denies because righteousness is the supreme law of human nature, the genuine interest of humans in enjoying and sustaining happiness. If we make our fortune by fraud or dishonest speculations, we would be ruined later. Hence, we become miserable after we make others unhappy. But if we are honest, we will prosper until the end of our life.

Our acts carry with them their natural, divine, or human sanction. We can enjoy our malice for a while, but sooner or later, if it is not our conscience that punishes us or the inherent justice of things, which is not an imagination but a fact, others will do justice.

To enjoy happiness, we must have logic and science of the mind, comply with psychological morality, general morality, individual morality, social morality, and social economy morality. When logic, science, and moralities are not repeated constantly in individuals or the life of nations, tragic histories repeat themselves. But, on the other hand, if logic and science and moralities are kept alive in the individuals or the life of nations, good stories are created, and individuals are prospering and happy. All we have to do is to follow history to see the truthfulness of this point.

Logic and science and all the morality types serve specific functions in life to make us aware of right and wrong moves and to choose the right ones to be happy. There are many categories of actions, and each has its moral, and logic and science are the tools to illuminate the moralities.

Logic and Science

Logic is thinking untainted by bias or emotion, and science is the intellectual and practical activity encompassing the set of principles that nourish and sustain the experience of happiness.

Sound logic and science should train our mind to understand that it would be better to position ourselves as ignorant than someone with false prejudices about life. As they say, absolute ignorance in the search for the truth alienates it less than the preconceptions that directly oppose it. It is hard for a preconceived mind which does not understand a topic to admit ignorance in that field. So, the morals, which are the lever to raise the reason to help the mind see its ignorance, are absent, and that is why, unfortunately, such a mind opposes the truth and will never be open to it.

The ignorant mind that wants to know, may understand that it does not know and is often disposed to receive the truth. Whereas people who have false prejudices believe they know and indeed they do not know. So, it is easier to make the ignorant accept the truth than to make people who have biases get rid of their erroneous ideas that they take for the fact.

Ignorance is the deprivation of knowledge or science. If an ignorant person is driven by a need to know, he can go forward on his own accord and receive it obediently, and he will see the truth. An ignorant mind is superior to a mind fed up with prejudices because, in the ignorant mind, there is a ready place for truth, while in a sense given to prejudice, the area is occupied by false ideas. It would be challenging to remove the biases to allow the fact to enter the mind and the heart. It is true that the mind or the spirit of the ignorant also has a ready place for what is not also true. Ignorant minds adhere to error because it was presented to them in the form of the truth. They fell into error for the sake of the truth.

In this case, it may be very challenging to reform the ignorant mind because they believe they have the truth. Therefore,

33

the reformation depends on the degree of the status, power, and authority of the institution that intentionally or unintentionally change a lie into a reality and make the ignorant believe it. The more powerful the institution which brainwashes the ignorant, the more difficult it is to open minds to the truth.

Factors such as pride, passions, laziness, weakness of mind, culture or poor education, environment, society, and clan that influence people may cause the development of their prejudiced soul. Ignorant minds have the power of freeing themselves from their ignorance if they have the will, whereas prejudicial minds cannot always be free from their little minds. That is why it is worthwhile for us to be the former than the latter because if we admit we are ignorant, there may be room in our heart for moral progress and happiness.

Remember that science, which contains logic, is knowing that we know what we know and that we don't know what we don't know, as they said. This attitude can help us avoid falling into the traps of the path as we progress through this life and not mislead others. As a result, we will have a happy life that will inspire others.

Psychological Morality

The animal neither believes nor doubts. But, on the other hand, the human being can believe in a supreme being or doubt because God, the Universe, equipped him with faculties that the animal does not have. But human beings have free will to use or develop those tools that God has provided for development or destruction. For instance, we can use our instinct and reason to believe, have faith in the light, or doubt; and if we are outraged, we can doubt for no reason and against any reason that will quickly drag us towards destruction. In other words, we will be an agent of destruction for society, making our world unhappy.

Some people may doubt without reason and against all senses because they have not used their imagination or intelligence to discover the truth themselves. Thus, to help arrive at a clear sight of the truth to find happiness, it is necessary, these people must have a minimum of disposition to accept the help, to remove the obstacles which hide the truth from them, to clear the stubbornness in which they are ordinarily enveloped. To paraphrase Blaise Pascal (Pensées, 10), these people will be better persuaded by their reasons than by those from others to accept the truth.

In any society, sincere faith in the light, the positive, God, is the base of all sound judgments of human beings and all its positive acts. Therefore, the primary function of faith is to establish the moral unity between humans without which no relationship would be possible, meaning that happiness would not be set.

Faith is necessary; it is a law for our mental and moral nature to make sense of life. Philosophy defines faith, generally, as spontaneous belief, which is compelling to our natural means of knowing, our reasons, our consciousness, and our comprehension. This conviction exists in everybody, but it differs depending on our passion. For instance, if we have faith in doing good deeds, we will do good deeds with all our mind, body, and soul, but if we have faith in doing evil deeds, we will do them with all our mind, body, and soul also. Know that the consequences will be different. When faith is genuine, it establishes the moral unity in us without which no relationship will be possible; it sets a toxic relationship in us when it is false. A false faith has the power to stain the heart, and knowledge will not enter the mind when it is not pure and clean.

Belief serves as the basis for all of our decisions and acts. For instance, the decision to be open to a particular knowledge class is connected to our beliefs. If we believe spiritual knowledge gives us light, we will spontaneously open to that type of expertise. If we doubt spiritual knowledge, we may close our mind to it; however, questioning higher wisdom that has the power to change our life for the good, it doesn't mean that we are not interested; it depends on the nature of our doubt. Peace of the mind and happiness are in science and faith in God, in certainty, which is the quiet possession of truth and knowledge. We are made to believe and to know, not to ignore or to doubt.

The essence of liberty, whether it is in a technologically or scientifically advanced society or not, wealthy or not, educated or not, regardless of race or gender, lies in power to choose in an infinite number of acts under the law, whether it is the law of God, nature, society, or the government. However, freedom has its limits. Freedom is not the power to violate the laws that have been put in place for our psychic, spiritual, and corporal happiness, but to act within the limits of reason, in good, unforbidden actions.

To think that we have the power to do what we want, and to believe that we can, with our wealth, the science of the world and its technologies always dominate and master the circumstances, it is to be mistaken; it is to be foolish and foolhardy. We will always remain human beings regardless of the value of our wealth, the depth of the world's science, and the advancement of technology. Therefore, we will have a miserable life if we choose the way of evil, and have happiness if we choose the path of good. Note that people will remember us according to our deeds.

If we do not have the freedom to obey the laws, we will never be happy. But ironically, if we had the freedom to disobey the laws, we still would never be happy, and we would make others' lives miserable. So, to be happy and make others happy, our freedom is limited to acting positively according to the laws.

General Morality

Moral responsibility is the character of individuals who must be accountable for their actions and receive the price for them. It is further defined as the moral necessity to suffer the consequences of our free actions if we are wrong or to benefit from them if we are good.

Responsibility involves the discernment of the good and evil principles, the idea of obligation. When we have the spirit of duty and feel obligated to do what we think is right and not to do what we believe is wrong, we feel a sense of moral responsibility. We cannot sustain our happiness if we lack a sense of moral responsibility, but we will be a fool if we think that we can be happy without moral responsibility. People devoid of moral responsibility have no wisdom and cannot enjoy their freedom; they cannot appreciate happiness. They cannot enjoy a good relationship, a good job, or their profession because they do not understand right and wrong. Therefore, to understand and abide by the moral law, we must have a certain degree and development of insight and spiritual education.

Exhibiting self-control in our life indicates a sense of responsibility. The consequences for responsibility are happiness if there is a gain in moral value, but if there is a voluntary decline in moral values, punishments are the consequences. We must develop wisdom to understand the limits of freedom. If we do not obey the moral laws, we will be irresponsible and miserable, but we are reliable if we follow the ethical rules.

Eventually, we will enjoy the necessary harmony of happiness and good.

Individual Morality

If we shy away from decency, modesty, honesty, optimism, and hard work, we automatically protest against moral life, and such an attitude is an outrage or threat to our happiness. What makes good people different from evil is their righteous life, the valuable life at the base of happiness and peace of mind.

To make ourselves and others happy, we must value moral life, respect ourselves and others. Such disposition requires a divine attitude, which separates us from the brute, making us the image of God, people who are not interested in seeking happiness in the wrong alleys.

Respect for ourselves and others gives a feeling of honor. When we are sincerely concerned about dignity, righteousness, honesty, respect for rights, the integrity of conscience, unity of life, and loyalty, providence automatically brings happiness to our soul, mind, and body. Such an attitude will make it difficult for others to look down on us, even if they hate us. We will be invincible in the battle for life, and it will not be difficult for us to sustain our happiness in this life.

Social Morality

A republic can only live and prosper, says Montesquieu (1896), by its citizens. It is the same for a family and any institution, which its members can preserve. The success of an institution depends on the virtue of the members, and when the republic or the institutions fail, nobody can be happy.

Practical virtue must be encouraged to guarantee the happiness of the members of any society. Without a minimum of morals and sound principles, no association is possible among humans. One of the critical virtues its members must develop for a republic and its institutions to prosper is tolerance, not indifference. The general goal is to bear that others may think, speak, and act differently than us. Tolerance implies no obligation, no surrender. On the contrary, it presupposes the persistence of the beliefs we may reasonably associate with others regardless of the difference (race, ethnicity, religion, gender) between us to have more happiness in our society.

Social Economy Morality

If our actions cannot make others happy, they cannot make us happy. In terms of Marcus Aurelius (Book VI, 54), what does not benefit the hive is no benefit to the bee. So, when we do something good for society to make others happy, we help ourselves as well. If we let this truth be front of mind, and put it into practice when we summon happiness, we will feel it.

Ah, the sweetness of happiness!

The sweetness of being happy is so great that even the wicked want to reach the state of happiness through illegality, immorality, or fattening. All the things that those ordinary individuals like using—Alexander Woollcott's terms, who was an American drama critic and commentator for *The New Yorker* magazine. The wicked always seek happiness in wickedness, ignoring the eternal truth that no path outside of moral laws leads to contentment. We may have an excellent personal income, a beautiful family, social status, good-looking physique, high social relationship, still, if obedience to moral laws is lacking, there will be no happiness. On the other hand, when we adhere to good moral laws, we can endure any hardship and develop a tolerance for each other and enjoy life.

The moral is to human beings, as water is to plants. We need morals to stay alive and grow, be happy, have a peaceful life, a functional family life, a healthy community, a prosperous society, nation, or world. As soon as individuals and institutions cut ties with moral laws, they will start going down like an airplane losing its engine.

So as many factors may influence different plants' water needs to grow or stay alive, such as being in an arid environment, indeed, many factors may influence our needs of moral values, such as a lousy environment, or economic hardship. The difference between plants and us is that we have the power to create a success story with our life to inspire others. And to continue to enjoy our happiness, we should share our happy story with others because we cannot enjoy our happy tale alone. It would be better if we had others, especially our inner circle, to show them that we have a successful story to inspire them, otherwise, a happy story is meaningless. What is the use of happiness if we do not have other people to share our joy with them?

Chapter 6

Do Not Rely on Perspective but Experience the Truth to Find Happiness

Once we are convinced and persuaded, the next step, a significant one, is to make a tremendous effort to not rely on belief only but experience the truth. Belief is the dimension that comes before experience. But unfortunately, most of us may brag about our belief in the truth and never make an effort to experience it, and we may never want to live the truth. So, we may pretend to believe in life and never experience life, fooling ourselves instead. As a result, we waste energy that should have been used for our advancement in promoting pettiness and living a hypocritical life. In such a case, how can we sustain happiness because we become the agents of corrosion of our lives and others? Therefore, we must strive to avoid being destructors programmed for that job.

But suppose we have the power to convince and persuade ourselves. In that case, we can go to the next level of understanding to believe and experience the truth so that others can see us as a living manifestation of it. Then, indeed, we will be a blessing to this world. If evil slays us, we will attain immortality; if we survive, we will enjoy glorification. Either way, we will win because we did our duty, and we will be happy, something the destructors will never enjoy, even if they accumulate this material world's wealth. They will always be in a cursed position to chase happiness, which they will never catch. They can see it but cannot reach it. These people's unrealistic chase of happiness will harden their hearts every passing day, which will bore them to resort to deceiving themselves and others.

We should strive to develop our inner life and use our patience when things seem sour. See any trials as an opportunity to create our story; do not let those who do not believe in truth drive us to despair by their negative actions. Instead, we should use our time to enjoy every moment of truth, whether alone or involved; know that no unbeliever can do that.

If we look for happiness, note that we will not find it from the exterior but from the inner. Therefore, we must understand how our inner world works and our composition to transcend the miseries and trivialities of this world.

Chapter 7

Our Composition

We are sophisticated beings. We are not bodies with personalities—only the ignorant think like that. We are a bundle of energy—intellectual, spiritual, emotional, physical, sexual, positive, and negative. Energy always wants to be manifested. Some of us may be urged to display positive energy and others negative energy, which may be combined to create different shades of construction or destruction.

According to the esoteric teaching of the Theosophical Society (see Purucker, 1972), we are composed of seven cosmic elements which add to each other to make us who we are. The seven elements are the sources of our powers, including our faculties, capacities, and physical strength. The first element is our Higher Self, our pure consciousness per se. The Self that is directly connected to the Universal one—to God. The Higher Self is the power that gives us the knowledge, perception, intelligence, and feeling or consciousness of Selfhood. The second element is our perception, which is the attribute or organ that gives us our spiritual consciousness and moral awareness. In other words, the understanding of ourselves, the knowledge of who we are, where we come from, and where we are going, awareness of the power of positive thinking and positive moral values, and awareness of the power and consequences of negative thinking. The third element is our reasoning, thinking, reflection. This attribute is the center of the ego-consciousness in us. The fourth element, our desire, is the driving force in our constitution. If the lower ego and our petty-mindedness do not corrupt our desires, we will develop the power to acquire pure knowledge, perception, intelligence, feeling, or consciousness in this life. Many spiritual leaders argue that desire is the source of human dilemmas in this life. They wrongly consider desire as exclusively evil. This property is neither good nor bad, according to esoteric teaching of the Theosophical Society. Desire is only such as our mind and our thoughts direct its use. We should never let our desires ride us; instead, we should ride them. When we take a ride with them, the best way to communicate with our desires is to hold our backbone straight (our mind), keep the reins tight (our thoughts), and always pull on the straps (our will) firmly for any deviation, and that is what our desires will feel and obey.

Our thoughts can spoil our desires like mud dirties pure water. When soil gets into clear water, it becomes dirty and cannot be used for drinking if not purified. Similarly, when negative thoughts, greed, lust, anger, and animal passion get into our desires, they become dirty and inappropriate for their original purpose, igniting the fire in us to become one with the Higher Self. Therefore, to filter out our thoughts, free them from greed, craving for power or money or lust so that our desires become pure, we need to focus our minds on positive thoughts continuously. Besides, a moral filter will help us avoid being prone to suffering.

We must practice contemplation of the mind, soul, feelings, and body to control our myriad desires and focus on the one that God has for us, our evolution. How can we do that? The Buddhist philosophy holds that mindful breath in and out is the first step to practicing contemplation. The in and out breathing practice is also the prerequisite to making the five mental hindrances pliable: sensual lust, ill-will, torpor and languor, restlessness and worry, and skeptical doubt.

The fifth element is the "Life Principle." This element is the "psycho-electrical field" manifesting in us as vitality; it is our breath, the breath of life. Our body's healing ability to take over illness depends on our profoundly relaxing breath work. The sixth substance of our constitution is composed of the model body, popularly called the astral body. The astral body is slightly more ethereal than the physical body. It is the framework around which the physical body is built and developed as growth proceeds. The astral body is formed before the body is created. It serves as a pattern around which our physical body is modeled and grows to maturity; that is why it disappears with the physical body when we die. The seventh substance is the physical body. The physical body is the lowest element of our composition. Although the physical body is classified as an attribute, it's not an "attribute" per se. It is our "carrier," it is like our house. Our physical body is no more an essential part of us than are the clothes in which our body is garmented. We should understand that we must value and protect the body not because it is our most important element but because it is our carrier. Damaging it is like setting our house on fire, and where are we going to live after that to continue our progression? So, use our common sense to protect the body; it does not require a lot of intelligence to understand that.

Although the physical body is our constitution's expression on the physical plane, we should not devote our life to its maintenance at all costs and completely neglect the other elements. Such attitude is equivalent to having a car and focusing on body maintenance while ignoring the engine. As a result, we will have a beautiful junk car.

According to the Bhagavad-Gita, our body is a field, our material object. We are the owner of that field of activity, and it does not own us. We are the one who should decide what to grow or let grow on it. This field of action can develop healthy or unhealthy products according to our will, inclination, and external suggestions.

It is not appropriate to identify ourselves with the field, our body. We should not be attached to our body because it is a property given to us by God to use for a limited time to cultivate profitable products for us and others. We will give back this property sooner or later. However, if we see it as our property to enjoy permanently, we will lament, be disturbed, and find fault in God and others, using Epictetus (*The Enchiridion*, I) language.

When the time comes for our dissolution, when we die, the divine part of us, rooted in the Universe linked with the All, will run back into that which is universal. We may believe that the dissolution of our physical body is the end of us because our mind is expressing thoughts from observation in this material world. For instance, we see people born, reach maturity, sometimes not, enjoy life or maybe not, and then they are no more in this world. They are not here to enjoy life with us in the full bloom of their powers. Each time we see or learn that someone passes away, we may lose our faith. We react by having frightening thoughts. Then, we reflexively inhabit the ordinary way of thinking about death. To cope, we may keep convincing and persuading ourselves that life is short, and our physical body must be enjoyed most of the time. Unfortunately, at the end of the journey, the last day in this life, we will realize that we wasted our lives because we did not develop the fundamental knowledge we needed in this transitory life for our evolution. Therefore, we never enjoyed our life because we did not understand the process of death, which is a change, a transition to another plane, another form of life, a dissolution of our components. All material things in this world are composite, not absolute, therefore, they must go through the process of annulment or death.

To sustain happiness, we need to control our fears. But, unfortunately, one of the sources of our fear is the dissolution of our body, which is inevitable. Thus, it is necessary to understand the process of death or why we will die someday to lower the level of anxiety that is constantly threatening our happiness when a circumstance makes us think about it.

According to the esoteric teaching of the Theosophical Society (see Purucker, 1972), the experience of death varies in each case, depending on our evolution and deeds. As deceased, we may spend a prolonged or short time withdrawing from the spiritual-intellectual and immortal parts of us. The withdrawal coincides with the breakdown of the seven elements of this physical incarnation. In the preparation by our consciousness to come in the invisible realms, our collapse proceeds through physical dissolution. This process may indeed be compared to the process of gestation when we were in the womb of our mother approaching birth into this material world, but here we are approaching rebirth in the next sphere.

Still, according to the esoteric teaching of the Theosophical

Society (see Purucker, 1972), physically, we die after the cessation of activity of the heart, and the last organ of the physical body to die is the brain. Although unconscious, the brain, and its memory, remain active for some time so that the Terrestrial Ego passes in review every event of the earthly life for a short length of time. While unconscious of everything else except this, our Higher Ego watches the entire motion picture of our terrestrial life that just ended, weighing every thought and action. Nothing is rewarding about cultivating negative or evil thoughts during our life on the earth. There is no doubt that we are winning when we choose to develop positive thinking during our life. Not only do good actions lead to our happiness as well as others' happiness, but when it comes time for our Higher Self to review the record of the good and the evil we did, the load of our good deeds will tip the balance to a higher evolution. The duality of good and evil in this world has its purposes. We come into this world to be tested so that we could be evolved to a higher sphere. If we stay strong and do our best to spread positivity, we have nothing to be afraid about death.

We should consider this world as a place we come to do our divine job, learn, develop ourselves, and help our fellows, and that we cannot stay here permanently because we have to go to our house at the end of the day to be with our Heavenly family.

Why should we be frightened of something inevitable like death, the dissolution of our components, which is a divine natural law? Are we afraid of sleeping? Unless we know that we did something wrong during the day, such as thinking and acting negatively, or doing evil things to others, and are scared of having a nightmare, we have nothing to fear. Similarly, if we are worried about our dissolution or death, it may be because we spent our life living in vain. However, if we did what is right most of the time during our life, we should have nothing to fear about death. Instead, we should feel liberated that we are going back to the source.

During the transition process, after the reconstruction of good and evil deeds is done, it imprints as a record on the fabric of the spiritual memory of the passing entity. Death comes at the end. Each element returns to its respective source. For instance, the physical body decays, and its atoms proceed to their natural attractions. The model body remains in the astral realms until it fades out bit by bit, along with the particles of the physical body. The "psycho-electrical field" manifested in us as vitality commonly called the "Life Principle" flies back to the natural reservoirs of the planet after our dissolution. And if we were faithful devotees to the Almighty, the process of our transition to the next life would start and be completed.

According to the Bhagavad-Gita, when passing away from this world, we come back in this world in spirit if we die in darkness or may not come back; we go back to the Godhead if we pass in lightness. If we were an unalloyed devotee of the Supreme Lord, we would pass in light, and we will go back to the source, but if we were not an unalloyed devotee, we would die in darkness and we will return into the material world.

Reincarnation, also known as rebirth or transmigration, is the philosophical or religious concept that the non-physical essence of a living being begins a new life in a different physical form or body after biological death. Traditional Christians believe that existence is not an endless cycle of life, death, and reincarnation to another form of life. Instead, they believe in one cycle: mortal human life, death, and resurrection to judgment. But some religions hypothesized that resurrection is a similar process in which a soul comes back to life in the same body.

In most beliefs involving reincarnation, the soul is seen as immortal, and the only thing that becomes perishable is the body. Therefore, the soul becomes transmigrated—passing the soul from one body to another after death—into a new infant (or animal). Then, depending on the extent of the individuals' reasoning development, they live again upon death to continue maturation (see Wikipedia).

God's original plan is to produce wholesome human beings. Still, most of us, from any cultural, social, and economic background, even spiritual, unfortunately, altered His plan by letting the illusion of this world deteriorate our reason to become inactive and chaotic, making it easy to perpetuate our foolishness.

According to Blavatsky, the cause of reincarnation is ignorance of our senses and the idea that there is any reality in the world, anything except abstract existence. From the sense comes the "hallucination" we call contact; "from contact, desire, sensation (which also is a deception of our body); from sensation, the cleaving to existing bodies; from the cleaving, reproduction; and reproduction, disease, decay, and death" (Blavatsky, *Isis Unveiled*, page 346).

Blavatsky learns about the mysterious doctrine of reincarnation from a few fragments of precious records of granite tablets and rock from Hindu remains in caves and temples. According to her, our development of reason plays a vital role in avoiding reincarnation. She explains when reason has been so far developed as to become active and discriminative, there is no reincarnation on this earth, for the three parts of the triune human have been united together. But the trinity has not been completed when the new being has not passed behind the condition of an indivisible spiritual entity or monad. "The immortal spark that illuminates it has to reenter the earthly plane as it was frustrated in its first attempt. Otherwise, the mortal or astral, and the immortal or divine, souls, could not progress in unison and pass onward to the sphere above" (see *Isis Unveiled,* pages 351-352).

According to the Theosophical Society (see Purucker, 1972), "[m]onads are spiritual-substantial entities, self-motivated, self-impelled, self-conscious, infinitely varying degrees, the ultimate elements of the universe." And according to Blavatsky (*Isis Unveiled,* page 352), the monad imprisoned in the elementary being cannot skip over the physical and the intellectual sphere of the terrestrial human and be suddenly ushered into the spiritual sphere above.

Does an irresponsible infant who died have to be reincarnated?

Again, according to Blavatsky, reincarnation is preceded by a violation of nature's laws of harmony. It happens only when the latter, seeking to restore its disturbed equilibrium, violently throws back into earth-life the astral nomad, which had been tossed out of the circle of necessity by crime or accident. Thus, in cases of abortion, infants dying before a certain age, and hereditary disease or cancer, nature's original design to produce a perfect human being has been interrupted. The immortal spirit and the astral monad of the individual—the latter having been set apart to animate a frame of the former to shed its divine light on the corporal organization—must try a second time to carry out the purpose of the creative intelligence.

Suppose we make it our duty to be always in the Lord's consciousness. In that case, we strive to observe the divine, the moral laws, and we become a mature soul, we would have a safe departure from this material world directly to the spiritual kingdom. On the other hand, if we spend all our life in the darkness, after the passing we might come back in this material world to improve our human ego.

Remember that our soul, our individuality, is, in essence,

immortal. Its development takes place on a descending and ascending plane by alternating spiritual and bodily existences. Reincarnation is the law of our soul's evolution. If we as a soul reach our perfection, we will escape this world after we die, and we will return to the Spirit, to God, in the fullness of our conscience. As when we, evolving souls, rise above the law of the struggle for life when we become aware of our humanity, so we will rise above the law of reincarnation as we strive to assume awareness of our divinity.

As souls, as long as we are not interested in the art of finding God in ourselves by developing the mysterious depths, the latent faculties of our consciousness, we will never find peace or happiness in this world, and the next.

Consider this world as a class we have to take and pass to go higher. That is to say, we come to the terrestrial sphere to learn, and if we do well, we go to the higher sphere. But if we do not develop our reason and discriminating faculties to choose to do good, not evil, no matter what, we will not be admitted to the higher sphere.

It is essential to be aware that great souls can be reincarnated too. Therefore, the Almighty can send them back here to serve as teachers to show us the good way. According to Pythagoras (see Schuré, 1960) and the Bhagavad-Gita, after millions of years of rest, the highly developed Reincarnating Egos or Masters may come back voluntarily to help humanity in a troubled time. Some of us may believe or not believe that, but those who have doubt, we should ask ourselves why the Christians are waiting for the second coming of Jesus Christ?

Our ignorance and lower mind make the weakest of the seven principles, our body, a significant obstacle that inhibits access to the divine life in this world. To transcend this body barrier is to be brave to take a thoughtful look at our body constantly. Contemplating the body is not for everyone because it is a scary reality that most people are not interested in and probably never will be. Nevertheless, the contemplation of the body is one of the ten contemplations we must frequently practice to achieve purity, overcome sorrow, end our pains and suffering, and open access to the correct path of knowledge and self-realization in this world (see *The Path for Deliverance* by Thera, 1959). This contemplation is often used as a concentration exercise to develop insight.

One of the best strategies is to start with the contemplation of the body first because it is the bondage of the body, the bondage of the material that prompts our feelings, mind, and soul to get contaminated by impurities such as bad feelings, greed, anger, and irritating thoughts. When we cannot get material things to satisfy our body, we are more likely to use our imagination to destroy our life. For instance, our morbid imagination can give way to the phenomena called the five impediments that will make our life undoubtedly miserable. As a result, we will be functioning as an unconscious entity in this world.

A simple way to start the contemplation of our body exercise is to be aware of our natural breathing process or rhythm. This contemplation activity can be done anywhere, at any time, if it is a quiet place. It does not matter if we are standing or sitting. In the process of breathing, we need to be aware of when we take a short inhalation or a short expiration or an extended inhalation or a prolonged expiration to start relaxing the function of our body. As soon as we feel that our attention is focused, we may direct our attention to the body. As we remain in the contemplation of the body, try to perceive how the body is formed, how it breaks down. Visualize the emergence and disappearance of the body: our body is here now, and we will get old, and sometime in the future, it won't be here. Convince and persuade our mind to become aware of this knowledge because it will help us to develop under-standing and a deep inner vision about the body. As spiritual beings, we are living independently, detached from everything in the material world, we remain in the contemplation of the body. Continuing the meditation, we are aware of the motion and the motionlessness of the body, clearly aware of looking forward or backward, clearly aware of bending and straighten-ing up, clearly aware of nibbling, drinking, walking, fulfilling the natural functions of the body. We are aware of standing, sitting, sleeping, and waking. We are conscious when speaking and remaining silent. Continuing, we should contemplate this body from the sole upward and from the top of the hair down to become aware that it is composed of skin stretched over it and filled with many impurities. And that our body consists of hairs of the head, hairs of the body, nails, teeth, skin, flesh, liga-ments, bones, marrow, kidneys, heart, liver, diaphragm, spleen, lungs, intestines, mesentery, stomach, excrement, brain, bile, phlegm, pus, blood, sweat, fat, tears, skin-grease, saliva, nasal mucus, oil of the joints, and urine.

We should examine our body with a detached mind like we were looking at an open sack, with openings at both sides, filled with various kinds of grain, with paddy, beans, sesame, and husked rice. And we examine its contents and see this is paddy, and these are beans, this is sesame, this is husked rice; we should do the same with our bodies to see its contents. Besides, if we are not blind, we admit that the content of our body is similar to the content of the open sack, so we con-sider and recognize the body. And further, we contemplate the body regarding the elements. Our bodies consist of solid, fluid, heating, and ornamental features.

And also, just as we should see a corpse thrown into the burial ground one-, two-, or three-days dead, swollen up, black in color, and full of corruption, we see a framework of bones, with flesh hanging from it, splashed with blood, and held together by the ligaments. Or a framework of bones, stripped of flesh, spattered with blood, held together by the ligaments. Or a framework of bones, without flesh and blood, but held together by the ligaments. We see bones disconnected and scattered in all directions; bones bleached and resembling shells; bones heaped together; after the lapse of years, bones weathered and crumbled to dust. So we realize that our own body too has this nature, this destiny, and cannot escape it (see *The Path for Deliverance*, §128). We are thinking of our own body, the bodies of kings or queens or presidents or millionaires, and we believe our body also has this nature, this destiny, and we cannot escape from it. Thus we remain in contemplation of our body and that of others or all together.

When the meditation on the body is developed, we will discern how bodies arise and pass away. We will make a clear distinction between the other principles and the body. This distinction will be present in our minds because of our knowledge and consciousness, and we will live independently, detached from this world. Hence, we will live in the contemplation of the body.

When we practice and develop the contemplation of the body very often to a point it becomes a habit firmly established, strengthened, and improved honestly, we will harvest many benefits. We will understand that we are more than the body. We will understand the necessity to be connected to the Supreme, the higher principle, to gain access to intuitive knowledge so that we can live happily. We will know that by making the body our top priority, we will never be free from the miseries of this world because the body is a fickle thing in which we cannot stay eternally. With such knowledge, we may be able to overcome pains at will because we will no longer allow ourselves to be overwhelmed by them; we may be able to suppress them as soon as they arise. We may be able to contain fear and anxiety because we will no longer allow ourselves to be overwhelmed by them; we may be able to subdue them as soon as they arise. We can endure cold, dry, humid, hot temperatures, hunger, thirst, wind, the sun, and the attacks of insects and reptiles. We can patiently endure harsh, harmful, or abusive words from enemies, friends, and relatives. We will develop invincible armor because offensive or harmful comments will not move us. We can endure intense, loud, bitter, unpleasant, or dangerous physical sufferings that assault us. We will understand that it is not worth using our energy to destroy others, a good relationship, and our lives to satisfy our body's cravings. We know that the body does not make the difference between us and others, whether we are tall, short, white, black, brown, yellow, a king, queen, or president. Our body is made from the same elements as any other body and cannot escape its destiny. What is important is developing the principles that animated us in the right direction. We have the power, the intelligence to rise, succeed, be happy, and be noble human beings independent of the body's condition.

From meditation on the body, we can understand that a weak, sickly, crippled body can have an elite intelligence, a soul full of vigor and energy, which can honor and benefit humanity because of the higher principles in action in a human. Pascal wrote his vigorous *Thoughts* despite continual suffering. For most of his life, Pascal suffered from ill health. According to his elder sister after his eighteenth birthday, he never lived a day of his life free from pain or some illness or medical affliction.

But his suffering did not prevent him from becoming one of the most influential scientists and mathematicians. For example, he contributed to hydrostatics the SI unit of pressure, the pascal (symbol: Pa). Pascal is one of the most influential authors of the French Classical Period. Another example is Napoleon Bonaparte, who was a French military and political leader who rose to prominence during the French Revolution and led several successful campaigns during the Revolutionary Wars. He was one of the greatest military commanders in history, and his wars and campaigns are studied in military schools worldwide. Napoleon's political and cultural legacy has endured, and he has been one of the most celebrated and controversial leaders in world history (see Wikipedia). And Napoleon had inherited cancer in the pylorus, which he kept all his life. Last but not least, Nicholas Saunderson (see Wikipedia) was blind and lame from birth and was a brilliant professor of geometry at one of the most famous England universities. When he was a year old, he lost his sight through smallpox, but this did not prevent him from learning arithmetic through assisting his father, John Saunderson, who made a living as an exciseman. As a child, he was also taught to read by tracing the engravings on tombstones around St. John the Baptist Church in Penistone with his fingers. In his early education, he learned French, Latin, and Greek. Next, a tutor taught him algebra and geometry, and later, he attended Attercliffe Academy, near Sheffield, for logic and metaphysics.

These people's lives indicate that they were more than bodies, but great souls in defective bodies that demonstrate the power of the Spirit. They lived in imperfect bodies, but the energy in them was beneficial.

Because of our knowledge and consciousness about the function, the actual value of the body, we can become comfortable with it, whether fat, thin, ugly, beautiful, or black. Once we sincerely develop such an understanding, we can experience at will, without difficulty, without effort, the four immaterial spheres or the four purifying ecstasies of the Divine Spirit and the celestial delight they may bring, here, in this world. The four immaterial spheres include:

- The sphere of boundless space.

- The sphere of boundless consciousness.

- The sphere of nothingness.

- The sphere of neither-perception-nor-nonperception.

Regarding the four immaterial spheres, the first arises through overcoming perceptions of forms, the second through the idea of space, the third through the notion of consciousness, and the fourth through overcoming the concept of absence of consciousness of space (*The Path for Deliverance*, §119-§125).

Then, we can develop the power to hear the celestial and terrestrial sounds because the body is no longer a barrier to our subconscious. We can build mind power to directly view other beings' hearts and read others like open books. We can obtain the memory of our previous birth. We can see people disappear and reappear, low or noble, beautiful or ugly inside, happy or unfortunate. We can understand how beings are reborn according to their acts. Set free from our passions, and we may come to experience in ourselves and this world the perfect deliverance of our soul, the liberation by our wisdom.

It is a well-known fact that there are connections between thinking, feeling, and the body. The body-mind connection is a concept fundamental to many belief systems. Because mind and body mutually influence one another, cognitions, the third principle, affect body states, and biological processes affect thoughts and feelings. So, it is necessary to practice contemplation of emotions, mind, and body for a useful life.

The purpose of the contemplation of feelings is to make us aware of our pleasant or unpleasant feelings and learn to balance our mind between unpleasant and pleasant feelings. When we reflect on our emotions, we can discern how our passions arise and how they disappear. We should be aware when we are dealing with cheering or sad sentiments activated by our mind. We know that we should remain independent and detached from our feelings because of our knowledge and attention. So, we linger in contemplating our feelings either in us or others to avoid violating our code morals to be happy.

In the contemplation of the mind, we know how greedy or unselfish desires, angry or kind thoughts, disorderly or orderly ideas are developed, and their effects on our body. We understand the thinking that is worthy or unworthy of consideration. We discern how thoughts arise and disappear. We are aware when we are thinking positively or negatively. We know that we remain independent and detached from vulgar, dispersed, and shameful thoughts because of our knowledge and attention. So, it would be best if we sojourned in the contemplation of the mind.

Sometimes, our soul may get trapped in sensual desire, anger, boredom, agitation, worry, and doubt because of some cravings of our lower ego and our body, but we should strive to see that it is not us. To free our soul from the unsatisfaction which causes our misery, we must enter into its contemplation, establish ourselves in the review of the phenomena called the five impediments: sensual desire, anger, boredom, mental agitation, and doubt.

When a sensual desire arises in us, we should be aware of

that and acknowledge that a sensual desire is taking over the mind and that this desire has nothing to do with the real us. Therefore, we do not want to be a slave of such desire because we did not summon it, and it is not appropriate. Also, we know that according to the ancient and wise Egyptians (see Schuré, page 145), "[t]hose who live as slaves of their sexual desire live in darkness," and such people cannot have freedom.

When anger arises in us, we should be aware of that and acknowledge that anger is taking over the mind. Most of the time, we get angry because others disagree with us. To paraphrase Ruth Bader Ginsburg, we should understand that when we react in anger or annoyance in a discussion, such a lack of self-control will not advance our ability to persuade or convince others. At other times we may get angry because people criticize us, which may be fair or unfair. However, there is no reason to get annoyed when others scold or do something wrong to us. A simple way to win the day is to practice serenity. Anger can destroy us and others, while peace can build our health and make us stronger. Practicing calmness gives us dignity. Anger makes us look like a fool. Being peaceful does not mean that we should not fight or defend ourselves, but fight with a dose of serenity, not anger. Fight with courage, not anger. Another way anger could arise in us is from the lust born from our passions and which can be transformed into anger later, according to the Bhagavad-Gita. For instance, when we have lusted after someone, and that person rejected us, we may react with anger and do something stupid that will ruin our life sooner or later as well as the life of that person. We may want unlimited power over others, which is not right because it is not practical to have such control. So, we will never have that, and as ignorant, we will develop tremendous angriness. As a result, we will experience physical effects, such as increased heart rate, elevated blood pressure, and increased levels of adrenaline and nor-adrenaline. We will never have serenity in such a case because it is a moral ill-will problem.

When we get angry, the consequences are a process, and we are like some beans, or potatoes, or rice, or vegetables in a pot filled with water placed on a stove. During the first couple of minutes, we do not feel the heat. Then, the water gets warmer, and quickly it gets heated over 100 degrees. With no power like the beans or the vegetables to get out of the situation, we will be cooked. Later, regrets and sorrows will eat us deliciously because we are their favorite food.

There are a thousand situations in life that could make us angry. Practicing serenity is the first tool to use to deal with any challenging situation we may encounter in our life. Therefore, we should strive every day to acquire a superior degree of serenity. Unfortunately, because of our past life, Karma forces us to come into this world with a temperamental, nervous, sanguine, or lymphatic dominance that we must be trained to overcome. If we are moody, we may act by a tendency towards anxiety, and it may become challenging to maintain our seren-ity. On the other hand, if we are tumultuous, we may have diffi-culty dominating ourselves under the effect of intense emotion. If we are too confident, we may get carried away or get angry and become violent when facing a challenging situation. Being passive inert in appearance may seem tranquil, but we may be predisposed to real erratic crises when setbacks are too long. To transcend our anger, we need to cultivate self-control. Many good books could help.

When boredom awakens in us, we should be aware of it and acknowledge that lethargy or negligence is taking over the mind. We should do our best to overcome boredom because of our knowledge about what such an impediment can cause in our life and others' lives. For instance, boredom can make us prone to react to events violently, irrationally, and immorally. Therefore, we need to maintain goodwill, a well-developed and perfected sense of morality to fight boredom.

When agitation takes over our mind, we should strive to be aware of that because we understand the difference between serenity and agitation. Therefore, we should do our best to orient our mind towards serenity by comparing agitation and calm. Furthermore, we should always realize that agitation affects our heart's rhythm and blood circulation. Therefore, we must think in a non-dispersed mode and avoid being part of any negativities.

Visualize the main benefits of calm. See the characteristics of usually calm people in fiery situations. The nerves and muscles keep a normal tone that facilitates all their physiological functions. When we are relaxed, we think straight. We do not get carried away for a long time in a problematic situation. We should make calm a habit that allows us to face any complex problem.

When we practice calm, we will not react to nasty words addressed to us. We will show impassivity because we dominate impatience, irritation, and anger, and will keep sufficient measure in the face of slanderers in our observations. We will strive to make ourselves uneasily invaded by the suggestions of anyone, only we will admit under the benefit of a thoughtful inventory the excellent quality of the affirmations or appeals addressed to us. We will let no one succeed in imposing a conviction without true certainty in obtaining a decision from us. We will show that we are not people over which a clever argument of a con artist will convince us because our presence of mind facilitates our vigilance to protect us. Unexpected events, setbacks, disappointments—inseparable in life—will not upset our equilibrium for an extended period any more than a sudden noise makes us jump. We understand that one of the best approaches is to move away from the annoyance source when facing a nuisance.

Without wasting our energies in lamentations or imprecations, we should coldly cultivate the necessary disposition to neutralize, as far as possible, unforeseen setbacks or disappointments, then spend the rest of our time at losses and profits. But, of course, no situation with seriously disorganizing consequences does not delight calm people more than nervous people. Still, relaxed people do not let it overwhelm them for long because they retain their confidence in their ability to pull themselves together and methodically regroup their means.

The worst adversities may affect relaxed people objectively much more than subjectively. Therefore, from day to day— sometimes from hour to hour—they go peacefully upstream, attenuating the evil that has struck them and endeavoring to overcome all the consequences one by one. As a result, they feel more vigorous and combative than before, and better armed for the fight, and they will enjoy happiness. If calm people have to face other battles, they will say they have seen many others; therefore, they often keep a modest attitude (see Jagot, 1951).

Acknowledge that it is the way life is—a battle to survive— and it will always be like that. There will always be opposition. The enemies will do any despicable thing, say any lie to destroy us, attempt to kill us, destroy our power, drag us out of control, try to convince our spouse to leave us for them. It is the dirty human game. It is sad, but it is what it is. So have faith in God and ourselves, invest in our self-development daily to develop our divine attributes; trust no others until they prove, to the end, that they have a righteous training, not people without a moral compass. Then, it will be difficult for us to get disappointed in life.

Remember that some people are like mosquitoes; they will never stop trying to suck our blood despite our efforts to stop them. We work very hard, and some people will try to steal from us. Do not get angry. Serenely, continue smashing the mosquitoes to prevent more of them from sucking our blood. We will survive if we continue to fight with the mosquitoes, not complaining that they are this or that. Please do not waste our energies complaining and telling them that their acts are despicable and that we condemn their actions and have no conscience. But, of course, they have no conscience. Can we give them one? They are not born to develop a conscience but to suck our blood.

It will help if we practice the contemplation of the state of restlessness, which is the reverse state of calm, either in ourselves or in others, to understand the drawbacks of such a condition and encourage ourselves to direct our thoughts towards calm. In other words, to develop an aversion for agitation.

In contemplating the restlessness within us, we will notice we are living in a state of neuromuscular constriction during the period of turmoil. If we spend our entire life in tumult, the form of compression will become permanent as continuous moral tension. This problem will affect our heart rate, circulation, and digestive functions, which sum up the chain of our thoughts. As a result, many pains and spasmodic manifestations will follow, contributing to our miseries and unhappiness about our life. Reasoning thinking may become difficult for us; therefore, we will think unconsciously, in a scattered mode. We may experience difficulty focusing on what is happening around us and what we are doing. We will be lost. We will feel tired even if we don't work too much. The cause of this fatigue will come from the fact that we are always more or less tense. Our attention oscillates between the rumination of the preceding hours and the expectation of what will come. The problem is that we are often meditating on issues that do not concern us, such as a lie in the newspaper, social media, or a stupid movie. We will become impulsive by definition; we will show ourselves according to the moment's mood or the tinge of circumstances, either overly rushed or unpleasant. Under agitation, we will become anxious, impatient with everyone, irritable. We allow ourselves to be carried away by language discrepancies, affirmative or negative excesses of which we will frequently see, but too late, the unfortunate effect.

Worse, under the influence of restlessness, it becomes difficult and almost impossible for us to communicate clearly with others. In addition, everyone will be uneasy around us. Even if we are silent, others will feel uncomfortable with us because of the irradiation of our spasmodic psyche. Under the influence of agitation, any talented agitator, fake apostle, or fake news can influence us because we are open to allowing ourselves to be invaded without sufficient circumspection to any discourse soothing our stress by some wrong perspective.

Without thinking, we will accept proposals and pass orders that could be regrettable. Unlike calm people, in the face of minor setbacks or disappointments, we will excessively disrupt our psychological balance for an excessive period. And suppose a genuinely disastrous event does arise in the little composure we have; in that case, we will react without lucidity or skill and aggravate the situation more than we mitigate the consequences. When the significant adversities of life present themselves, we will sometimes suffer not without courage but rarely with the impassibility that would allow us to coldly consider the tactics to be followed to overcome the affliction (see Jagot, 1951).

The calm is the cubic stone, the pedestal where we must stand, unshakable if we want to conquer ourselves, overcome adversities, and have a happy life. Thus, we remain in the contemplation of the calm and the agitation because of our knowledge.

When doubt has invaded our heart, we should know that doubt is in our heart, and we should remind ourselves that doubt is the basis for failure of any decision or resolution we may take to grow and develop ourselves, to recognize the truth that can free us. The degree of our distress depends on the nature of our doubt. If we create a rational doubt, a temporary suspension of judgment between an idea and a refutation that presents explanations of equal value, it would not be difficult for us to recognize the spiritual truth when delivered to us and studied. It is because the suspension was inspired by prudence and a sincere desire to find the truth. When we are oriented toward a rational doubt, we do not want to make mistakes or look like a fool. For us in this category, what is doubtful must be studied because it may be true or false. Then, after examination, we will accept or reject it. Such doubt needs to be balanced so it does not become an impediment. In other words, we should not spend our entire life studying the truth. The danger is if it is prolonged, such doubt can become our intelligence. A good judge knows when to make a verdict, so be a good one.

If we develop a methodic doubt, which is one of the conditions of thought-out science, it might be more challenging to grasp the truth. When we have methodic doubt, we have doubts because we believe that our senses sometimes deceive us; therefore, we cannot be sure that we are not being deceived at any particular time. So consciously or unconsciously, we may use the system or stages of doubt of Descartes to try to find the truth. Such suspicion may make us think that only uneducated people believe things that are not true, so we want to be sure that we do not fit in this category and that we are awake. We want to be sure that malicious demagogues are not deceiving us because there are many false prophets and gurus. Deep inside, we may know that God exists, but we believe that we cannot rely on God's omnipotence and goodness to ensure that we are not deceived, as it is apparent that we are sometimes deceived. Therefore, our attitude about truth may sound like skepticism, but it is not. We somewhat believe, so we must be very careful, and behind our methodic mask, we may not have the life we were born to live. It is challenging to make us believe, but possible. If exposed to a convincing, persuasive, methodic argument about the truth in addition to life trials, we might accept the fact.

Unfortunately, suppose we develop an unnatural, irrational doubt, consisting of doubting to doubt, stagnating in doubt as an end, and a final state of reason, so in that case, we live all of our life in a state of sickness. We doubt for the sake of doubt. Irrational doubt inspires us not to be interested in the truth, period. Therefore, no facts, nobody, no tragic events, nor providence can convince and persuade us to see the light. No material relief will bring us peace when our mind is infested with irrational doubt. It would help if we struggled with ourselves to triumph over any doubt about the moral value presented to us to the point of bringing the mind to align with it.

Belief serves as the basis for all of our decisions and all of our acts. For instance, the decision to be open to a particular knowledge class is connected to our beliefs. If we believe spiritual knowledge gives us light, we will spontaneously be open to such a type of knowledge. On the other hand, if we doubt spiritual understanding, we may close our minds to it. However, for some of us, questioning higher wisdom that can change our life for the good does not mean that we are not interested; it depends on the nature of our doubt.

Peace of mind is in science, philosophy, and faith, which is the peaceful possession of truth, as health is the smooth mastery of life. God created us to know and believe in his plan, not to be an ignorant and faithless mess. Know that we are naturally endowed with the will to learn and understand the purpose of life to develop faith. It is not vain to have such natural desire— the natural desire to gain knowledge and to comprehend the truth. "Our understanding," says Bossuet (1836), "is made to find the truth. Our composure and supreme happiness lie in accepting and keeping the truth. Our thoughts are an active faculty; its normal state should not be the inertia implied by irrational doubt but the work of researching and developing an open mind required by the conquest of truth."

Faith is a necessity, a law for our mental and moral nature. Peace of mind begins with the belief in the understandability of God's plan for us—the design of our evolution. If we do not have faith, it will be impossible for us to have a positive mind. Irrational doubt is our worst poison. From any point of view, doubt has disastrous consequences in our lives. Doubt can cause chaos in our mind; it can foster selfishness in our heart; it can lessen our character; it can spur us to be disgusted with our life. We cannot live on doubts, negativities, or negations. Living without faith is like having no power to boost our life, while every action in the mental and moral order, as in the material order, indicates a limited capacity.

A prerequisite for us to be interested in developing morality and to know or become aware of ourselves is to focus our will on a daily lifestyle that is a meaningful expression of the life of continued growth and development. Once we embark on such an endeavor, we are no longer ignorant, and we might be immune from the five impediments because we know what they are. We understand that these impediments are not in us, as the wind is not in the sky. They are passing or transitory. They come and go. It is when we associate with them that they seem to be part of us. As the sky is never associated with the wind, acknowledge it and let it pass to always stay serene after a storm. We should never be associated with the impediments. Only be aware when they are present in us and do our best to overcome them and let them pass. When they come back repeatedly like the wind will always come again and again in the sky, we should continue to overcome impediments until they die.

We should be aware when we are free from these five hindrances in the contemplation practice. Because of our knowledge and attention, we know how to overcome them when they are present, and we know they will not rise again once they are defeated. We understand the power of sensations. We know how they are born and how they die. We know how our perception forms and disappears.

Because of our knowledge, we know the troubles that may arise from our dependence on the senses. We understand how sensual problems begin and disappear, and we know when we overcome them, they will not reappear. We know when we are fully aware and when we adhere to the law and when pure energy, joy, tranquility, and serenity exist in us. And we know when they do not exist and how they are born and disappear. We understand what suffering is, what causes pain, and how to put an end to our suffering. We know how phenomena arise and disappear because of our consciousness. We understand what real heroes and divine people are. Heroes and divine people do not die for defending their bodies or lusts because they have a deep understanding of their bodies and the endless suffering lusts can bring to life. Heroes and developed people understand the material form. They know how they are born and how they disappear. Instead, they choose to die in defending great principles to advance humanity, make others enjoy a better life, and make us aware of the purpose of life. Therefore, we should be thankful to them and live by them, not the celebrities who care only about their bodies.

We are here for our progression; we have to stand in the correct seat of this world, and that is why God gives us will, intelligence, and a mind. The only way to make our mind, intelligence, and soul stand in the correct seat of this world is to walk on the positive side, and we should strive to know ourselves and understand the principles in us. Once we stand in the correct seat, we will experience more happiness in our life. Do not fool ourselves, be aware that we will encounter some bad moments once in a while. Remember that this world was not made to be a paradise free from problems. Like the electricity we have in our house, the light will go out for a while when some bad weather hits our home, but know that it will be restored. The blackout is for a moment. Each time we are experiencing dire circumstances, remember Marcus Aurelius' (Book IV, 49) genuine pieces of advice to "[b]e like the headland, on which the waves continually break, but it stands firm, and about it, the boiling waters sink to sleep." Being like a headland means that we should not cry out "why" when facing adversities. The headland never cries out "why" the waves continually come and smash its feet because it knows the waves are doing the job they were brought into existence to do; the headland knows deep inside its position is to stand firm.

Using Marcus Aurelius' language (Book IV, 1), the sovereign power within us comes from cosmic principles. It is the fire our Creator put into us to master any difficulty that may fall into our life. The tests are necessary because they are the materials whose divine task is to make our fire brighter. For the sovereign power within us to be efficient, to neutralize the opposition, the problems, the evils, the diseases we encounter, we must have the maturity and a pure heart and be sincere to ourselves. We have three choices on the battlefield of life. If we develop our strength and acquire genuine knowledge to progress, we will survive, which means we will be fit for the glory. If we build our wickedness, we will be the material, the opposition, the problems, the evils, the diseases which the sovereign power within others that are strong will encounter. If we are weak and choose to be the faint of heart, we will give up when we meet the opposition material because we do not believe in the divine fire inside us, the sovereign power within us. To be sincere to ourselves is to know where we stand. Did we spend most of our life developing our strengths or making ourselves and others miserable? Indeed, we are naturally endowed with the sovereign power within. Still, suppose we do not nourish it with positive imagination or pure heart. In that case, it will never be manifested when we need it to defeat the opposition, put evil out like fire devours the materials which bank upon it like an obstruction to leap higher and higher out of those obstacles. Therefore, we need to develop a fire attitude because, like the fire needs obstructive material to grow, we need opposition for growth.

How can we manifest the power within, and how will we be sure that it is effective and working for us? One of the things needed is to begin to spend our time knowing ourselves, knowing the principles that govern us, and striving to understand their functions. Also, we need to develop a firm conviction and an intense resolution that we are a mini-universe. We have the power to overcome difficulties. Chu-His (Chan, 1987; Medhurst, 1975), the great Confucian commentator, supplied adequate testimony for that argument when he said, "Heaven an [us] are not properly two, an [we are] separate from heaven only by having [a] body." The conviction and the resolution can only be developed when we keep practicing the contemplation of the sovereign power, the spirit within us in action to a point it becomes a habit firmly established and strengthened. A simple way to initiate the contemplation of the sovereign power within us is to be aware of our natural breathing process or rhythm, and then visualize a pure, bright, beautiful fire devouring an object while the fire is leaping out higher and higher. Then, imagine the sovereign power within like the pure, bright, beautiful fire burning our problems. And it would help us if we convinced ourselves that this too should burn to increase our strength. The enormous advantage of such a practice will be that each time turmoil comes into our life, the sovereign power will automatically take over them. Note that if we do not recognize the sovereign power within us or do not develop it, we are getting into the habit of focusing on the negative, which will manifest in spades in our life, hence spiritual death!

The point of these contemplations is to discover that we are not our body, feelings, and emotions. We are not our personality, our lower ego. We are more than that, we are a spirit, and when we stop to identify ourselves with them, we will be happy. We will experience the joy, peace, and serenity beyond this world in our gut. So, we will remain in the contemplation of the spirit.

Once we understand who we are and the process of life, we may develop respect for life. We may be able to see divinity in every human being. We will understand that when we let our evil side take over and destroy other living beings, that is cruelty, and we cannot experience happiness. When we are addicted to committing cruel actions, through such activities, according to Buddhism, we fall into a low state of existence, a woeful course of life, into perdition, or hell, and we are more likely to have a short life in this world or the next life (*The Path of Deliverance*, §30).

Chapter 8

The Three Worlds and the Mind

The divine, intellectual, and physical or material worlds significantly impact our happiness. It all depends on where the will (motivation, Spirit), the principle (source, cause, foundation) of our acts, commends the mind to reside and travel. The mind can fantasize about anything, but the act will not happen if the will does not want what the mind fantasizes. But, on the other hand, any action the will wants to happen, the mind will go along with to make it occur. For instance, if our will is sincerely interested in divine affairs, if it wants to reflect in this world the will of God to manifest good and prevent evil, our mind will inevitably be oriented toward that purpose. If our will is oriented toward intellectual activities only, such as scientific, literary, or artistic activities, our mind will be turned toward that goal. So, the will to acquire knowledge will make the mind interested in learning. However, if the will is interested in worldly, material activities, the mind will get involved and wrapped in mundane material concerns. Therefore, our journey in life will be off of the divine path, and we will be traveling up to the dead-end course of life.

According to Hermes-Thoth (see Star, 1888), through the will, the mind sees the phases of life unfold. The eyes of the will enlighten the Spirit. According to the Bible, in the beginning, God said: "Let there be light!" and the light flooded infinity (Genesis:1-3, NIV). But if it were in God's will to let darkness continue to surge endlessness, we would have never gotten light. The point is that regarding the choice between the good and the bad, positive or negative, we are free to choose according to our will, but we are not free to choose the outcome. If the eyes of our will are directed towards the good, or the truth, we will see the truth shine, and we will get the happiness we desire. But if it is towards evil, or lies, we will experience miseries. Therefore, we must turn our will towards good, justice, and truth so that the phases of our lives are less turbulent.

If the will is interested in constructive activities, the mind will entertain positive actions; if the will is interested in destructive activities, the mind will entertain vicious acts. The mind will always follow the penchant of the will, our own accord. The mind is the source of the conscious, the cognitive. In the divine world, our consciousness has no boundary with the consciousness of the Absolute Being. Because in the heavenly world, the Absolute Being's consciousness and ours are one, as the consciousness of the Almighty, our mind can see and possess the three terms of all the manifestations: the past, present, and future. Therefore, when our mind is aware of our past, present, and future, what we did, what we are doing now, and what we will do, we are certainly on the rising path of progression.

In the divine world, the mind is free to develop its power because it has the full ability to balance its energy using active intelligence and absolute wisdom. As it resides in the divine world, the mind has no interest in pettiness but in exploring the perpetual and hierarchical realization (awareness or understanding) of the virtuality (essence) contained in the Absolute Being. It is inspired to be interested in the universal law, the regulator of all manifestations in the unity of substance, mastering the science of good and evil.

The influence of the divine world makes the mind clearly understand the consequences of actions. There, the mind knows the reward of good ideas and the punishment of evil thoughts. Any good action is creative and always brings happiness, and any evil act is destruction, bringing unhappiness sooner or later. The influence of the divine world makes the mind aware of this because it is dignified in the heavenly world.

In the divine world, the mind usually has complete, absolute control over its faculties and is, therefore, said to be "self-possessed, self-conscious." A human being who possesses such a mind will develop a complete notion of the percipient consciousness from the worldly, exterior, or even mental concerns or attributes. Such a mind will be preoccupied until "its" becomes the undivided consciousness. Like the Supreme Being, such a mind contains and could emanate the infinite creative possibilities in the Absolute Being's environment.

The main interest of the mind in the divine world is to build muscles to facilitate the domination of the Spirit over matter, to become the motor of the principles animating beings, the principles of all force since the mind comes to the understanding that the Spirit is the only reality. That matter is only its inferior, changing, transient expression, its dynamism in space and time. Therefore, a mind under the influence of the divine can make its owner in this lousy world, right here, a spiritual entity who is unbreakable, a divine-spiritual life-atom. The essential characteristics of such a soul will be harmonious.

The intellectual world is a world of ideas. In the intellectual world, the mind's task is to realize ideas. The intellectual world is where the mind manifests, realizes (brings into concrete existence) ideas as the contingent (dependent, subject of the Universe, God, the Absolute, the Higher Self) by the quadruple work of the mind: affirmation, negation, discussion, solution.

According to Brady (2020), "An affirmation is a foundational means by which we create our reality, structure our worldview, and confirm our beliefs. Every day, knowingly or unknowingly, in the form of affirmations, we give our subconscious mind instructions about who we are, what we can do or be, and what our life means." Through our daily habitual ideas, we can affirm God's existence, manifest the Higher Self or, the lower self, love or hate, depending on whether our mind is placed in the divine world or the physical world. Through affirmation, the mind may manifest ideas that deal with unity, the principle and synthesis of numbers. Our progression depends on unity because we come from the One, the Absolute Being, the master Soul. Through affirmation, the mind can bring scientific ideas into manifestation, which gives the mind perception to see things, visible and invisible.

Negation is the process by which our mind may cancel a concept. For instance, negation can cancel the idea of evil's existence or God's existence, the Higher Self or the lower self, love or hate, depending on whether our mind is placed in the divine world or the physical world.

Discussion is the activity by which our mind may debate. For instance, the mind may review the idea of God, the Higher Self or the lower self, love or hate, evil to convince or persuade itself.

The solution is solving life's problems or dealing with life's issues, which are inevitable in this world because they are necessary for our progression. In the world, existence is very complicated, so there are no easy solutions to life's intricacy. Looking at what is going on in the world, the injustices, miseries, turmoil, and sufferings caused by others seem unnecessary. For many, especially the non-believers, the pessimists, the question of God's existence is a problem. It depends on the capacity of our intellect, our will, mind, knowledge, and spiritual training to find the answer to whether or not God, the Higher Self, exists to solve the problems of our existence.

Suppose the will wants the mind to focus mainly on the material world. In that case, it will concentrate accordingly. Thus, the individual will fully experience the secular world's good or evil, depending on the being's education, knowledge, or morals.

As a human being, a relative being, we are the synthesis of the manifestations of life in this material world, called to rise, by an eternal expansion, in the concentric spheres of the Absolute. Therefore, the intellect is the appropriate tool for the task; it must be constantly engaged in the divine affair, not wasted in mundane matters.

We come into this world as an aspirant to be a divinity. Still, the overwhelming pressure of life and lack of knowledge of many people make this world also a training ground for evil instead of purely a training ground for aspiring gods. The material world is a dense forest of illusion, which constantly suggests that all powers come from it and that there is nothing beyond it, and we have the impression it is real life. This impression may make us believe that our look, countenance, money, and house are compelling, which may make us determined to do anything, destroy or deceive others and ourselves, to damn our soul for a good look, countenance, or money.

Yet, the material world has the power to create an illusion

but never force us to believe in its deceptions. We use our own free will to believe in its false impression, and we become a demon contender instead of a god aspirant, which is our ultimate task. The material world impels, but it does not compel us, meaning that it produces inspirations but does not force us to follow its impulse.

Do we want to have a happy life? If so, we must aspire to be a divine person. Take upon ourselves the responsibility to make our brothers and sisters discover the virtues that this world contains. On the other hand, if we do not want to reduce miseries, take upon ourselves the mission to be the devil to inspire others to discover the evils that this world encloses.

If we aspire to be divine, we are courageous; we have hope, the daughter of faith and the mother of charity. But we should develop circumspection, the manager of our acts, because the world is so malicious. Strive to be the master of the science of the mind and believe that happiness can be achieved by intelligence, the submission of the lower cosmic principles to the work of the Higher One, and we will not be subject to great disappointments, catastrophes, reversals of position, ruins, falls from high places, pitfalls, ambushes, and perils and destruction by enemies.

We should always be aware that there will be no end to good and evil in this physical world. The fight between good and evil will never pause. Nature's job is to germinate people's acts that proceed from the will. Some people will develop good inclinations in their life, while others will develop ill tendencies. No one can change that. People with good intentions would like to be leaders, and people with unhealthy preferences will want to be leaders too. Nature is impersonal. It is like a machine, give it a material to weave, and whatever the colors of the material we present, it will create something without asking any questions, and we will get a product with that color. Give to nature happy color, and we get delighted products, give to nature sad color, we will get miserable products.

Every action always produces a reaction, a response, sooner or later. For example, if the science of truth and love drives our will, we will enjoy a healthy, happy life; on the other hand, if the science of evil and hate inspires our will, we will experience sickness, miseries, and sudden death.

Nature will work out any inspiration from us, communicated by the vibrations of the astral fluid. We have the freedom of action in the circle of the universal law, but we do not have freedom from the consequences of our actions as stated before. For instance, to make it easy to understand, we have the freedom to eat junk food, but we do not have freedom from the consequences of eating junk food. If we develop a culture of bad eating habits, we should not expect a healthy life. Freedom of action is a test in the circle of the universal law. It is a test given to the soul in this world to see the actual will of the soul. If we have children and don't give them the freedom of action, we will never know the original will of our children. Human beings are too personal, it is tough for most parents to do that, but God, the Universe, is impersonal. God wants us to develop our divinity, and real divine people balance the antagonism of natural forces or law, linking effects to causes.

As aspiring divine beings, we should understand that when we violate natural law, a sudden fatal result will occur; in contrast, when we break a moral law, the violation will grow into the four results the Tibetan tradition describes (see Mcleod, Ken. "Karma As Evolution" article): full ripening, the result from what happened, the result from what acted, and the environmental consequence.

Full ripening means that sooner or later, our actions will germinate into something that will affect many aspects of our life. If the act is correct, we will experience peace, joy, tranquility, serenity, and prosperity. If the act is immoral, destructive, or harmful, we will experience suffering, chagrin, and moral pain. Deriving from our evil actions come pain, despair, grief, sorrow, and premature death, and more likely than not, our loved ones will have such an experience. Whatever acts we commit, our acts will mature, and we will reap the fruit of our actions, whether directly in this life, in the next life, or one of our future lives. Hence, the outcome of full ripening is the projected experience we established in a good or immoral action.

The result from what happened means if we act ignorantly, we will probably never be free from suffering, we will never be happy; we will ruin our life and the lives of others as well. But if we are acting like savvy people, we will be free from suffering, and we will be happy; we will bring joy to others' lives.

The result from what acted signifies the consequences of our actions on us. For example, suppose we are constantly functioning according to the moral law. In that case, we will develop a predisposition to do the right thing in every circumstance, which will become a habit, a pattern of behavior, a second nature for us. But, on the other hand, acting continually in disaccord with moral law will predispose us to perform consistently in a wrong way every day of our life.

The environmental result signifies our actions will shape our environment one way or another. For example, taking pleasure from helping others and manifesting great respect for life will create a prospering climate. In contrast, our evil intentions will create a destructive environment.

It will make a difference later in our life if we start developing moral values and self-development before our old age. La Bruyère (2004) said, "most people spend the first part of their life making the other miserable." We should not spend our time doing things that will make our old age miserable. For example, suppose in our teenage or early adult age we were not interested in developing courage, good inclinations, good physical habits, and that we were indulging only in pleasures. How could we expect to be happy in old age? In such a condition that does not mean there is no hope for us, but we have to have a lot of courage to reprogram our mind and heart with transcendental knowledge in our old age to reverse our situation. Miracles are possible, to paraphrase William Blake (1797), only the people who hold miracles to be ceased puts it out of their power ever to witness one. At any time in our life before old age, if we do not let ignorance take over our lives, our old age will be peaceful.

We should be wise to use the prime of our life to choose virtues over vices, whether or not we are under the proper guidance from parents or school. Do not let our weaknesses prevail, do not follow the wrong crowd, this will lead to regret and bitterness that will consume our old age.

Use our young adult age to strengthen our mind to guide us to understanding how to love the beauty and severity of discipline. Learn about the prodigious power of our will, which, if skillfully trained and exercised, has an infinity of positive applications on our body, our soul, and our environment. But if we choose to let our will be unskillfully trained and do not exercise it properly during our prime age, it will have infinitely harmful effects on our old age and our environment.

In the Karma concept, our choices during our young adult age develop a trunk, which gives rise to many ramifications and leaves with time, then sweet or the bitters fruits. Galatians (6:7-8, NIV) confirms that "[d]o not be deceived: God cannot be mocked. A [person] reaps what he[/she] sows. Whoever sows to please [the] flesh, from the flesh will reap destruction;

whoever sows to please the Spirit, from the Spirit will reap eternal life." So, before we feel sorry for those who had an unhappy life in their old age, find out first about the orientation of their will when they were in their prime of life, the ancient wisdom from *The Book of Thoth* says.

Suppose our actions have their law and particular purpose. So, a general rule must govern their development, which creates specific consequences if we do not follow. And this is because of the severe logic that connects actions. Our foolish actions will always have fatal repercussions in the future. Therefore, the genuine orientation of our will, moral development, in our young adult age largely determines our happy existence in old age as well as our loved ones' happiness. The instincts and faculties we develop in youth will mature in our old age. Therefore, it is salutary for us to sincerely surrender to the Law of God, the Universe, at an early age.

There is a position where we can still retrace our steps off of the path to our destruction. However, we will need the will to realize the truth in our mind, virtue in our soul, and purity in our heart to do the task. The only danger is that once we cross the point of destruction and go too far, it is difficult to come back, and the final destination is decrepitude and eternal death.

It is worth understanding that the mind is also an avid traveler that likes to take breaks to the other worlds if the will allows it. Suppose the will permits the mind to visit the intellectual world while dwelling in the divine world. In that case, exposure to the intellectual world ideas or activities will illuminate the mind. A divine intellectual mind will be developed. The result will be the same, but to a lesser degree, when the mind resides in the intellectual world and is often vacationed to the divine world. When the mind lives in the heavenly world and often goes to the physical world, exposure to the physical world or physical activities will develop a mundane divine mind. Such a mind will be focused on enjoying the material world, possession in the name of God, or glorifying God, and will be happy if it is sincere. But if the mind is not genuine, it will be a pretender and enjoy fake happiness. The world has a lot of pretenders, such as pastors, who are very good at preaching the gospel, inspiring others but are very shady. They are sleeping with others' spouses, stealing the congregation's money to be happy in the name of God. The result will be the same, but more unfavorable, when the mind resides in the material world and often vacations to the divine world. The problem with this category of mind is the lack of exposure to the intellectual world, which can illuminate the mind and inspire prudence in directing the will to avoid the disappointments, the pitfalls, the ambushes, and the perils of the material world. When the mind resides in the intellectual world and frequently travels to the material world, a material, intellectual mind is created. Such a mind may be for sure an atheist. If a genuine will guides the intellect, although the mind may be an atheist, a non-believer, it may be an optimist, otherwise a very pessimistic mind. The result will be the same, but to a higher degree, when the mind resides in the material world and often vacations to the intellectual. When the mind lives in one of the three worlds and frequently moves to the other two, it may be focused on the enlightenment of the material world in productive material activities to make the material world a better one. Depending on where the mind resides, the sincerity of the passion for making the material world a better place will be higher or lesser. The mind cannot live in the divine world permanently, without traveling to the other worlds, especially the physical world, because of the irresistible pleasures of the senses that attract the mind.

It is not difficult for the mind to permanently reside in the material world and never travel to the other ones. In this case, the will may be blinded by the material world, and such a mind may have no consciousness of judging a situation, no vision. A mind that never leaves the material world to visit the other worlds may be unethical in the whole meaning of this concept. A worldly mind will be very pleasing in its corrupt state despite the warnings of a life of punishment, torture, perpetual captivity, violent death, or suffering. Such a mind has no circumspection, which is the director of the acts, no science, and sooner or later, in the end, the soul who possesses such a mind will be lost in the abyss of infinity. The sad part of such a mind's existence is that it may believe that it is creating and transforming the material world while causing great destruction in this world. Such a mind is not fertile because it does not make any situation for the soul's evolution; it does not create to transform the soul, stripping the lower personality, shining the Higher One.

The mind can be exalted in the divine world and maybe dignified in the intellectual world, but rarely ennobled in the material world. In the material world, the mind is hampered by innumerable powerful temptations. A mind focused on material gain cannot appreciate the power of the spiritual, moral domain. Therefore, it can only be destructive.

People's minds that are not directed by the science of the truth, the love, and the willingness to do good, the realization of their acts and work will destroy them unexpectedly.

When we understand that we are more than a body, our inner eyes will be open to see and experience the three different worlds simultaneously in this temporary world. We will work on our character and circumstances to find tangible meaning to live as a god and keep fighting and moving forward to our evolution. We will be able to sustain inner happiness instinctively.

When we are aware of the effect of the three worlds on the mind, many advantages can be obtained, for instance:

1. We will no longer be something the material world can easily split because we transcend our naivety.

2. Our mind may be less disoriented when experiencing temptations, difficulties, and evil because we can place our mind in the proper sphere with the assistance of our genuine will.

3. Troubles may sidestep our strength of mind despite our knowledge. Still, we will control the problematic situation sooner or later or prevent the worst scenario from happening because of our will and faith.

The will must agree with reason to develop a strengthened soul and mind to improve our personality. An essential part of us is neither our assets, knowledge, nor talent, but the strength of our soul against bestial passions. The power of our soul must be built from the harmony of reason and goodwill to create a noble character in us. The qualities of that character are righteousness, justice, kindness, genuine ideas, noble sentiments, good wishes, and all of the virtues that balance and coordinate the powers of the strengthened soul.

The strengthened soul's will energy is unshakeable in its designs, in fidelity to itself, to its convictions, to its spiritual values. It is an intimate force with its world, constituted with godly principles that motivate and guide its acts. Such a soul makes its conscience more valuable than its opinions. It gives more importance to duty than to interest. It places its conscience above utility and does not seek to please at the expense of responsibility and has no fear to displease so as not to fail.

It loves the truth and does not worry about popularity but self-esteem and people whose esteem is worth something. The conviction of the strengthened soul's principles makes such a soul superior to events and has the power to rise at will above fears and hopes. The strengthened soul can create fortunate circumstances because of its firm faith. The strengthened soul's resolute will and faith and constant striving to let reason and love of justice guide its daily life in dealing with others, give the soul no time to be unhappy and make others sad.

We have to strive to strengthen our soul to bring light to our world, our character, and other people's worlds. We can start by saying, "Let there be light," like God said when his will wanted to bring light in the Universe, and there was light (Genesis 1:3, NIV). The meaning of light here for us is happiness. We are superior energy made in the image of God's power, so we have the authority to say, "Let there be happiness after a bad experience," and may happiness overflow in our life, around us. We should develop an open mind and use a mixture of our will, humor, and imagination to create and sustain our happiness in this world.

If we have a genuine will, we will see the light shine in our environment and the happiness we seek. Desiring happiness is our right. There is no need to deceive others and ourselves to realize the achievable because such desire is possible. And genuinely wanting happiness is already creating it. We should always hope for it to come to life if we know how to combine productive actions with rectitude of mind, making desire fruitful.

Nothing can resist a firm will that loves the truth and justice. Wanting what is just and fair and fighting to ensure its realization is more than a right; it is a duty. Therefore, be resolute and ignore the problems that may be in the way of our happiness.

Chapter 9

Be a Diamond, Not a Graphite Type

Diamond and graphite are crystalline forms of pure carbon. It is said that graphite is the poor miserable cousin of the wealthy happy diamond because of the fundamental differences in how the carbon atoms are arranged together. In graphite, the hexagonal structure of carbon atoms is set in long parallel sheets that easily slide past each other, which makes it soft and can be easily broken by our fingers. On the other hand, diamond crystals are a tight-fisted network of carbon atoms securely held in four directions, endowing the diamond crystal with great strength, making it the hardest naturally occurring mineral in the world.

We can find an analogy between the internal arrangement of carbon atoms of these two cousins, graphite and diamond, and the arrangement structure of our thoughts. Like the different structure of the assemblage of particles between graphite and diamond make the diamond a hard substance and the graphite a soft one, our collection of thought systems can produce the strongest, the noblest, happiest being, or the feeblest, vilest, lowest being in the world.

Besides the analogy mentioned above, there is a fundamental point or way in which diamond's internal working and graphite's internal working and ours are different. The interior arrangement that produces the hardness of the diamond and the graphite's softness naturally occurs under the heat, the pressure of earth's surface. At the same time, we are endowed with the willpower to create thought structures for the good or the bad to develop a moral or immoral personality under the heat and the pressure of life, circumstances, and our environment to be happy or miserable.

Our arrangement of thoughts traditionally can be grouped into two main categories, spiritual and mundane. Still, since our beliefs are constantly being influenced by circumstances or Karma, the spiritual and the mundane may affect each other to a great extent. The spiritual may be the dominant factor, or the material may be the dominant note. Like in music, the composer arranges the notes to create a tone that may be full of or lacking in warmth to make a beautiful melody. The point here is that we have the power to choose the arrangement of our thoughts. Beautiful and ugly thought structures are not naturally occurring in our mind. Instead, we create or allow life events or environments to produce them. How our thoughts are structured may make us develop a divine personality or a mundane personality. In the former case, we are determined to realize ourselves and inspire others to become aware of the great virtues of creation. While in the latter case, we are preoccupied with satisfying our worldly desires, degrading ourselves, and inspiring others to become aware of the vices of creation.

The arrangement of our thoughts can make us a diamond type, someone that no events, no evils have the power to break, or a graphite type, someone that insignificant events or adversities can break, or downgrade easily. Events and others can inspire us to arrange and rearrange our thoughts. We should be conscious and aware of controlling how our ideas are being set to sustain our happiness in Karma.

Without developing a strongly-held network of spiritual arrangement of thoughts, experiencing and sustaining happiness in this world is merely an illusion. And if we believe such a structure of thoughts is unnecessary and that material possession and power are enough to make us happy, we are merely a cheap pretender. So how can we develop a compact and strongly-held network of spiritual arrangement of thoughts like the network of atoms in a diamond to sustain our happiness in this world? A simple way is to know ourselves, give an excellent orientation to our will, and develop good moral values. We must be a transcendent person to be happy in this world. So, our happiness depends on how well we know ourselves, our will, and our moral values.

We will be better off if we use our imagination to create a thought system that could encourage us in sustaining our happiness, which could help us develop a diamond's mind, not a graphite one. For instance, observe nature; let it be our teacher to establish such a mind. Consider the following thinking: the wind is in the sky, but the sky is not in the wind, said the Bhagavad-Gita, so the wind never affects the sky by its actions. Notice that after a hurricane, a tornado, the sky is as calm as before the development of the wind. If the sky were in the wind, the wind would have never come and gone. Both would have gone, or the wind would have been there permanently in the sky—similarly, lust, anger, fear, and evil desires may be in us, but we are not in them. That is why they come and go like the wind in the sky. Therefore, like the sky, we should not get disturbed when they arrive; have faith that sooner or later, our calm will be restored while we are taking the necessary steps to resist until they leave. When we bring such a thinking structure while experiencing any difficulty, we are more likely to come out as a victor.

Chapter 10

Be Smart, Do Not Let Evil People Wipe the Smile Off Our Faces

The cosmos is composed of light and darkness. We are a miniature cosmos. Like the Universe, we have light in us—such as our intellect, reasoning faculty, positive emotions, and love—and we have darkness, such as negative emotions, discords, vices, hate, and follies. Therefore, our primary task in this material world is to achieve unity and harmony in ourselves. And know that when we accomplish this mission, God will descend into our consciousness, then we will participate in the Universe's power and make our will the stone of the hearth, the altar of God, the throne of God. Then, we will achieve wholeness.

It requires a lot of work, patience, self-control, courage, and a lifetime to achieve unity, to become like God. Everything comes from God, but to test our will, God gives us the freedom of action in the circle of the universal law. If we choose to be unwise or a wise person, God will reward us according to our will. God gives fools deceitfulness, arrogance, and evil power to do violence to survive and be miserable. In contrast, God gives wise people knowledge, wisdom to endure in this world and be happy. It is not worth being jealous or angry when we see fools seemingly prospering if we are in the intelligent camp. Fools' prosperity will not last long. Longing for evil is to enslave ourselves to destruction. A perverse, evil mind is the beginning of suicide. To spend our life being evil is dedicating ourselves to the eternity of death.

We should be patient and believe that knowledge will help us survive, and the more we overcome obstacles, the more we will grow in power. According to Kant (1975), knowledge is a cooperative affair in which both mind and object contribute, and the reason contributes to the relations while objects contribute the logical connection that proceeds.

Thus, both mind and life contribute to the development of our knowledge. Likewise, our mind contributes to what we and others experience in life and makes a sound or unsound connection of the consequences that urge us to act in a certain way. To develop the proper knowledge, our mind should ask the appropriate questions in life during the experience because nature will answer accordingly. If we ask a question to find the truth, we will get a truthful answer. On the other hand, if we ask a question to justify our ignorance, we will get a solution that will perpetuate our ignorance.

We should use our knowledge to unite hope ceaselessly with our faith no matter how painful the suffering caused by the fools of this world. To suffer is to gain knowledge; pleasures dissipate and impoverish. Any pain accepted with obedience and resignation is accomplished progress (see Star, 1888). Such an approach does not mean that we should not fight to protect ourselves from others' evil. It would help if we understood that an evil person could take the form of any bad thing. For instance, they may develop a mind like the smallest, threatening, appalling creatures in the Universe like a virus mentality to destroy others for the sake of destruction.

Some people view doing evil and destroying others as an achievement. The difference in the achievements between good and bad people is that reasonable persons will say let God's will manifest here and do the necessary for that to happen and be proud of their accomplishment. On the other hand, the evil people will say let destruction manifest in this world and use their energy to make that happen and be proud of their achievements. These people will be so proud and delighted to wipe any smile off our faces.

And know that nothing—philosophy, gospel, education, magic, or remedy—can change them because of their natural mode. So, we must protect ourselves if we want to sustain happiness in this world, and to be able to do that, we must constantly be on our guard even when we are socializing and playing with some so-called friends. Most of the time, with friends who are craving for money, power, or attention, they will not hesitate to set up traps for us to trip on, and if they succeed in their effort, they will expose us by forging something about us because they have a malicious soul.

We should be wise, not be naïve, open our eyes when doing business with others to prevent being hurt because many people in this world are deceitful. Many people are indeed good and have good intentions, which may inspire them to deal honestly with us. Nevertheless, many people are evil too. That is, they have negative values that may inspire them to deal dishonestly with others. Most people are variable, erratic, and they can take a set of possible values ranging from negative limitless to positive limitless. For instance, some people might exhibit exceedingly simple actions one hour, one day, and another hour or day, indicating incredibly deceitful and corrupt actions. They have the capacity but are not interested in realizing unity to become like God.

As human beings, at any given time, depending on the circumstances and the extent of the spiritual development and self-development of some of us, we may be oriented to positive values or negative values. So, we should be wise when we are dealing with others. We may not honestly reveal ourselves to others for personal purposes, trying to conceal our shadows during a situation. Yet, in our quest for good friends or spouses to be happy, we must be good ones for the truth so that others can live through us. And always remember that we cannot be good friends or spouses without loving the truth. To go further with this thought of Saint Augustine (1864), which means that if we do not love the truth, we cannot be capable of friendships and that the love of the truth is the condition, the cause, the origin, the foundation of harmony, and as a result, happiness. On the most sacred level, marriage, having a family, if we don't like the truth but lie, we won't be able to be good spouses, fathers, or mothers, we will have dysfunctional families—hence, a life filled with miseries.

The truth is what is, and the lie is what is not. If we don't like the fact, how could we love someone, our spouse, or our children? For instance, regarding wife, without makeup, the elegant clothing, and all the rehearsed polite manners when we were dating for the seduction game, in the house, in the everyday bed, she is what is—the true her. But, if we liked the false her, the lies, we wouldn't like what we see after the marriage. Likewise, regarding husband, without the fancy suits and the flowers, the sweet talks during dating, in everyday life after the wedding, he is what is—the true him. But if the wife enjoyed the false him, there couldn't be love when living together because the illusion is fading away.

The person who does not like the truth does not like anything because of the inability to love. Therefore, if we don't like the truth, it will be challenging to love ourselves. Truth and love complement each other because they are part of moral, both of them are positive, while the lie opposes both of them because it deceives and corrupts.

However, in unusual instances, it is permissible to lie. It is legitimate to lie to protect ourselves and our loved ones from our enemies, but not to lie to satisfy our lust, our greed, or to deceive others. The prophet Abraham in the Bible is a good illustration. Abraham moved on into the region of the Negev and lived between Kadesh and Shur. For a short time, he stayed in Gerar, the kingdom of King Abimelek, and there Abraham said of his wife Sarah to the king, "She is my sister." He lied to King Abimelek to save his life because he knew in the king's kingdom, if someone's wife is beautiful and the king wants her, they will kill the husband for her. So as soon as Abimelek learned that attractive Sarah was the prophet's sister, the king sent for Sarah and took her. But God intervened and said to [Abimelek] in a dream, "Yes, I know you did this with a clear conscience, and so I have kept you from sinning against me. That is why I did not let you touch her. Now return the man's wife, for he is a prophet, and he will pray for you, and you will live. But if you do not return her, you may be sure that you and all who belong to you will die." And the king listened to God and apologized for the offense against Sarah and returned Sarah to Abraham (Genesis 20:1-14, NIV).

The rationale behind Abraham's engagement in the deception is clear enough. Given how ruthless royalty could be in the ancient world when it came to beautiful women, Abraham was sure that his wife's beauty would put him in danger when they arrived at a foreign dominion. This lying was a rational lie, a legitimate one in the eyes of God, which is why the Almighty did not rebuke his prophet for lying and came to the couple's rescue. Abraham did not lie to satisfy his lust, greed, or deceive the king for personal interest.

So anyway, there are actions we think that people will never dare do. We are greatly mistaken if we have such belief because some people will dare to do the despicable in our face, even the sovereigns and presidents. If we have any doubt, read the crime section of any major newspaper or watch a particular program about crime on television. Remember, this world is the training ground for good and evil, and those aspiring to be trained for good and to be happy should protect themselves, so do not be too trusting. Be wise in our business dealings with others. Like Jean-Paul Sartre (1972), the French philosopher, said, "Hell is other people." Use our understanding to find out about the inner characteristics of other people so that we can identify them and discard them in doing business deals to sustain our happiness. Note that any individual can be among the other people. The other people may include relatives, friends, co-workers, etc. We may be the other people, too. Please, there is no need to be paranoid. Live! Be aware that we are living among human beings and that some of them can act dangerously, and do not get angry at them. Forgive them because they do not understand, as Jesus Christ said. According to the Bhagavad-Gita, their mode of nature makes them demoniac.

No matter how wise we are, some people will find a way to fool us. Control ourselves because there is no reason to get angry when people disrespect us or do something despicable. Their words or actions define them, not us. Such people empower us to develop a sophisticated mind. So, appreciate them and be happy! Controlling our minds will make the world less dangerous than most people believe because we become transcendent people!

Chapter 11

Living or Dying By a Few Individuals

Our primary duty is to live before we die. So, traditionally, eating healthy, being physically active, resting, keeping ourselves clean, and having a suitable connection with others are proper rules we must observe to live. We abide by these rules, not because they are easy to follow but according to nature and good judgment. These are merely good actions that will keep us living. Note that we do not live by those mentioned earlier alone, but also by others. We need the constant inspiration of others to live.

To live is the act of existing (not dying, destroying, degrading) with life. To live is to pass the time, our existence, in a noble, superior manner, develop good habits, conduct, or prospering conditions to grow in mind, body, and personality. One of the ways, manners, and habits we can grow in mind and character is to be creative, be worthwhile. To have a good life is to live through good models, guides, geniuses, and heroes. So, the poet Marcus Annaeus Lucanus, better known as Lucain

(Pharsale, V-60 env. Ap. J.-C.), is right when he said that humankind lives by a few.

It is good to choose to live through wise people but wrong if we live through unwise people. The latter action is equivalent to dying. Everything about noble living is for humans who have the will to live, not self-destructive people, the greedy, lusty people interested in satisfying their low desires. For them, living (which is indeed dying) is the act of destroying, degrading life. If we follow good characters, geniuses, real heroes, and good-hearted people, we live by them and will not have a miserable life. While if we are following the ones who only believe that they are no more than their physical body, we are dying by them, and we will have a miserable life.

We can choose to live by the upright geniuses, thinkers, artists, legislators, philosophers, heroes, and saints who inspire to develop good inclinations to advance humankind through the stages of evolution. Or, we can choose to die by the twisted geniuses and pessimistic philosophers who inspire us to have a sick, destructive life. It is up to us.

When we decided to follow intelligent people, we did that not because they are wise but because it is reasonable. "Happy life depends upon being reasonable, and this alone" (see Seneca, *On the Happy Life,* chapter II). On the other hand, when we choose to follow unwise people, it is not that they are foolish, but because we are unreasonable.

Marcus Annaeus Lucanus was somewhat correct because a few groups of humankind live by the few moral leaders, while a majority group of humanity is dying by the amoral leaders. It is not distorted to say that more people in the world are dying by the few bent idols they follow; that is why divorce, adultery, dysfunctional families, drug addiction, and alcohol addiction is widespread nowadays. Unfortunately, some of us cannot see the lack of divine creative and constructive imagination of our idols. We should understand that great leaders inspire to achieve greatness, evolve, and increase understanding to enjoy a genuinely happy life. Whether in literature, philosophy, sciences, religion, education, medicine, politics, or military, everything great leaders do is for the good of humankind, and by so doing, inspire to live amid tragedies that are inevitable in this life. Indeed, the people who have common sense admire and follow such people, living through their creative and constructive imagination. They do not follow unwise people. Fools believe in their fake strength and do not understand that they are not immortal. Their foolishness may be so glorious that they are proud to flatter themselves and think that they can support the shock of any events while working on their doom. Because of their folly, everything is conspiring against them, and they are the only ones who ignore it. So, if we want to live, we should not live by them. Fools live by the fruit of pride, imprudence, or willful faults. We should not be associated with anyone who has no will to cast off their destructive passions and errors and inspire us to improve ourselves so that the key to happiness will be given to us.

Instead, we should live by idols who can inspire us to turn on the ray of Divine Light from the occult sanctuary to help us dispel the darkness of our future to see the way to happiness. Then, people who want to live will follow leaders who can make them understand that when they do the right thing, whatever happens in their life, they should never break the flowers of hope, and they will reap the fruits of their faith.

If we believe some people are exceptional, we will admire and worship them. They will influence our behavior and thinking. If they are wise people, we will have a meaningful life; on the other hand, if they are not responsible, we will have senseless lives because we will mimic their lives, which does not make sense to them. Hence we will live through the former and die by the latter because we are connected spiritually with our admirers. At first, we may not see the effect of the influence of people we worship because the activities of their power are not visible; it is beneath the surface of life, the material world. We cannot see the whole picture of our transformation at first when we follow them. Gradually, we will be transformed by those we admire.

The spiritual aspect of life is a fact, but sadly, many people do not take it seriously because material life absorbs them. Also, they are powerless to shake their naivety. The power of transforming lives is in the spiritual, not the material. The material is just a manifestation of what we want to be, to have. Our situation today is the result of our past actions. So, likewise, our future will be the result of our actions today. There is an invisible weaving, not an imaginary one, that makes our acts germinate.

When we are aware of what is happening behind the veil of life, we will make only wise decisions to seek the company of or admire people who will genuinely uplift our thoughts to a higher level to open the gateway to happiness for us. We will be interested in the lives of people who show that everything is possible through the power of God, and our faith will increase tremendously. Although we have a model, we will not be dependent on it because it will teach us how to be ourselves, not to be a puppet who mimics another material puppet addicted to superficial things that will hinder our development.

One of the best decisions to make is to avoid living by people who have a history of manipulating words and actions to suit their own selfish needs. If we do, we are not applying ourselves in the right way, and we will hardly achieve anything good, and our evil actions will hurt our life and others who may look to us for a model.

We do not need to be intellectual to determine when we live or die by the few. We will feel growing, prospering, joy, love within, satisfaction, and healthy when we live. Beautiful things will happen in our life. If we live by the real heroes, saints, scientists, philosophers, artists, and writers, we will feel the genuine inspiration to develop harmony in our life. Soul-to-soul relationships, the good parts of them, the rational ones, will minister to us, enabling us to move and sustain happiness to live.

We will live because they encourage us to pierce the limited consciousness barrier and benefit ourselves to have courage, develop nobility, unselfishness, and higher wisdom. But, when we are dying by the few, we will feel hate, despair most of the time, and we will have a penchant to destroy. We will feel negative vibrations, emptiness. We will become prone to losing our nerve quickly, making us an incendiary entity. We will grow inner anger. We will never find happiness. We are dying because they inspire us to limit our consciousness by the illusion of the material world, lust, anger, and greed. They will not encourage us to keep up and develop. They will inspire us to be content with our limited consciousness and be preoccupied with cherishing the body out of regard for the soul or develop the vulnerable parts of us, the irrational ones.

Each second, minute, hour, and day we are at the crossroads of our life because we have to make a decision, and each decision we make can be either beneficial or damaging, wrong. So, it is essential to think carefully. We have to pick the right idols to live by to affect our life and live to progress positively. The right choice means that we admire the real heroes, saints, or we were firm to listen to our inner voice to respect them. If we make the wrong choice, we will experience a harmful effect, which will mean that the false idols inspired us; we were weak to listen to them. Whether good or bad, there are always invisible activities behind our actions that make them germinate and have beneficial or dire consequences. Therefore, be interested in living by the few upright leaders who distinguished themselves from the shady ones by the power of their will to develop a healthy creative imagination. Live by leaders who create a beneficial character and image by their goodwill and dare to play a divine role in accomplishing something that advances humanity towards scientific, spiritual, philosophical, social, political, educational, and material progress. It would be best to live through the upright few because of their inspiration to expand our will to fight for good. But, even if endowed with an instinct for originality, a desire for the best, we may, first of all, let outside dangerous twisting forces influence us. Under the spell of these hostile forces, we may disdain such salutary few for a while, but in the long run, when we regain our common sense, we should follow and appreciate them.

It is well known that during hard times, when members of a nation willingly depend on the few who show moral quality, strength, and intelligence, a "State" sooner or later escaped ruin and progressed to become established and gained the respect of other countries. Examples of this are Rome under the leadership of Marcus Aurelius, Europe under the influences of the intellectual and philosophical movement in the seventeenth and eighteenth centuries known as the Age of Reason or simply the Enlightenment, and the United States under Abraham Lincoln, Franklin Delano Roosevelt, and Dr. Martin Luther King, to name a few.

But when members of a nation depend on the crooked few who are experts on demagogy, their countries went down and lost the respect of other countries. A good example is Haiti and its demagogues, which was the first black republic in the Western Hemisphere and now is a failed country and the poorest one in the Western Hemisphere. The successes or failures of nations are primarily the successes or failures of their leaders endowed with or deprived of the instinct of originality and great vision.

Humanity indeed lives by a few, but it is also true that humanity can die by a few. Society needs initiators, guides, political, social, and spiritual leaders to walk the path of moral, social, scientific, and spiritual progress. But in this era, only a few follow these guides. The majority, unfortunately, live by the ignorant idols who cannot free themselves from their sufferings because they are slaves to their woes.

But we should know that nothing is imposed on humankind without their consent, whether it is wrong or right. Others have no power to impose their imagination on us without our permission. For instance, we predispose ourselves to choose based on our practices, our routine process of choosing the correct or beneficial answers that will solve our problems, or accepting the false solutions that won't. So, admitting and denying the fact depends on our routine.

We need to be aware of what we constantly practice in our life because what we force our minds to repeat over and over will be difficult to make our minds give up, even if it is a wrong idea. To illuminate the power of our routine in choosing in life, let's use a little math here. To internalize the correct answers of the four basic operation tables when we were kids, every day under the tutelage of our teacher, we had to go through the training process of repetition, especially under the old system of education: one and one make two, four minus two equals two, three times three is nine, four divided by two equals two. Once we learned and internalized our four basic operation tables, if someone told us one and one make two, we automatically agreed with that person because we knew deep inside ourselves that this was the correct response. If someone says that one and one make four, we automatically disagree with that person, and we may laugh because we know that is not the correct answer. If we had a lousy teacher who falsified the tables to make us, for instance, believe that three times three is one, one times one is four, and so one, we naively keep repeating the wrong answers religiously. We will disagree with anyone who told us otherwise. Even if someone shows us the tables with the right answers later, we will not accept the correct answers because our subconscious has already internalized the false answers.

It is natural for anyone whose mind has been training rigorously for so long about an ideology, a philosophy, a culture, whether beneficial or unbeneficial, to believe and be ready to fight anyone who thinks otherwise. From repetition, under the instruction of a good teacher, the mind makes the correct connection of two and two make four, three times three is nine. Also, from repetition, under the instruction of a bad teacher, the mind creates the wrong connection of two and two make ten, three times three is four. By analogy, the repetition of listening to upright leaders or rabble-rouser leaders will make the truths or the lies slip into our subconscious, and the facts or the lies will be released on-demand later. As a defense mechanism in arguments in life circumstances, the truths or lies will become automatic for us. Unfortunately, if we adopt lies for the defense mechanism, we will be doomed, and there is no question about that end. Therefore, we should never forget Kwan Yin Tzu, the Divine Mother Asian Buddhist bodhisattva's warning (see The Tao-Teh-King Chapter X footnote). "It is necessary for attending to the affairs of life to be very careful of those thoughts which appear insignificant and trifling [those little subtle lies others keep whispering in our ear], lest they find a permanent lodging in mind. If they are retained in the heart, there is a disease in the vitals, which no medicine can cure." We should use our intelligence to discriminate between leaders to follow.

The choice of following unwise people, which may destroy us, is not the right action for our efforts, for, by nature, we want to live. Consequently, when we choose to follow either wise or unwise people, it is either a right or a wrong action; it is not in the people selected, but the efforts to live or die through these honorable or dishonorable people, using the languages of Seneca in *On the Happy Life* (Chapter XII). Therefore, the good or the bad involved our choice and not the people themselves.

Chapter 12

Through the Noise and the Haste, Find Time and a Way to Develop Ourselves

Nowadays, with social media, many people are more than ever delighted in airing their opinion by making a lot of noise about a matter they have no sound understanding of whatsoever. Such people are merely fools who consciously or unconsciously manipulate our mind to confuse us to have control over us, to look important. In addition, because of their disdain for moral values, they act like high school teenagers, spending their time bullying those they believe are weak for fun. In the hands of people who cannot control themselves, social media is a tool to hurt others and erode relationships.

These powerful communication tools can be appropriately used only in the hands of groups who are subject to reasoning action, responsible individuals in the moral sphere, in their relations to others. The users should be people of knowledge who are aware of the power of their thoughts, character, and psychological states. Users should be conscious of the difference between opinions and the absolute truth. Why would we follow fools who find no pleasure in understanding but delight in airing their own opinions (Proverbs 18:2 NIV)? The noise of the fools has the power to cause unpleasantness or great disturbance in our quest for happiness. Besides the social media noise, anything that cannot contribute to our self-development and the progress of our environment, including the so-called leaders, pastors, educators, false relatives, and friends, are pushing on us and should be considered noises. So, do not let this world's noise undermine our self-development.

Another obstacle to our development may be the hurried lifestyle of this world that is taking control of our life and which we may not be aware of. It would help if we had control over the pacing of our life. When a cadence, a tempo is playing all day in our head, eventually we are likely to get into the rhythm, consciously or unconsciously, and dance, and come to the point of non-return. Suppose we get jammed into the haste of this world. In that case, we are more likely to forget about our self-development and give priority only to material progress and to be individuals before our time. Hence, it would be challenging for us to focus on our self-development.

Strive to find time to develop ourselves through the noise and haste of this world by cultivating calm, taking time to know ourselves, understanding our Creator's plan. By itself, the calm powerfully offers protection against noise and haste. But, in the process, we must have self-control, meaning that cultivating self-control is essential to acquiring an imperturbable calm.

Be resolute in maintaining our impassiveness despite the noise and rush that can annoy us and distract us from our goal, and we will succeed in our self-development. This endeavor must be done with relentless effort, by an application of all our time.

Here is a simple approach we can consider in making time to develop ourselves through the noise and the haste of this world. The best way to start improving ourselves is to learn how to feel our true self. We cannot develop something we have never experienced. We have to feel it first, and then we take the divine feeling beyond this world and continue wanting more of such an experience.

As Barbarin (1952) suggests, at night while lying in our bed on our back waiting to fall asleep, especially while experiencing insomnia, eyes closed and hands clasped, clear our brain of all thoughts. And then get into a state of complete muscle relaxation and imagine that our body is dead. Relax our body to the point that it merges with the bed. Keep a relaxed breath, at ease, not thinking about a short or long breath, just breathe freely to relax our physical body, any restless emotions to quiet them. Keep our mind quiet, still, calm, serene to feel the peace of the Self, to feel the real us, which is the Higher Self in us, the Spirit that animates our body. Do not think about our body. Free our mind not to feel it, as well as our personality, the greedy little ego, the cause of all our troubles. We are so detached from our body, lower self that we are not even aware of the problems of this world. So, spiritually distinguishing our lying personality, body, and the Higher Self, the Spirit in us. Assume we are hovering over our body and seeing it as something foreign. The point here is to dissociate the real us subjectively and the vehicle God gives us to operate in this material world and that we worship so much that we do not even know we exist. This exercise aims to open our mind to see that we are not our material body, which prompts us to act most of the time immorally. This exercise should allow us to experience the difference between living totally in the body or being concerned only about our body and living in the Self.

The difference is divine peace beyond the peace of the material world, the liberation.

Another time we can also complete this experience is when we wake up feeling depressed about what is coming ahead of us during the day. If we do this exercise every night before going to sleep or every morning before getting out of bed, we will feel less unhappy in our life. Making a course into the invisible world like that, not in the supernatural form (which is dangerous and complicated), indicates a genuine understanding of solving what escapes in our material judgments.

Chapter 13

Open the Mind to the Truth to Develop Consciousness

Consciousness is a form of energy; it is the state of being awake and aware of our situation. Even though we may have an outstanding mundane education, we may be unconscious of who we are, where we are right now, where we are going, what we know or do not know. Hence, in Buddhist terminology, we can be categorized as ignorant because we do not understand the purpose of practical knowledge for our happiness and progression.

There are many reasons for such handicap—being unconscious. A fundamental one is that we may not have an open mind, crucial to developing consciousness. Our mind may not be open to the truth because it is blinded by our petty-mindedness and the influence of the constant buzzes of some institutional lies in our ears. As a result, we develop an atrophied consciousness. Furthermore, our lack of consciousness may make our mind rebel against any unfamiliar truth, making it difficult for us to work on our progression and see the spiritual connection between causes and effects, good and bad Karma, moral and immoral.

Another reason is that we may think we are saved because we are a church member or a preacher. How can we be saved if we lack awareness? Suppose we discarded other intellectual-spiritual knowledge unfamiliar with the theology we used to listen to or preach and believe that such knowledge is dangerous. However, that knowledge is in good standing with positivity. How could we have inner development?

We must open our mind to the truth to develop our consciousness. Not that consciousness cannot be developed in one day, one week, one month, or a year; it may take many years, even a lifetime. Awareness is something that needs to be practiced and continuously developed. This task requires the development of intelligence sustained by a constant firm conviction. A steady spiritual belief cannot be acquired by watching only soap operas or reading merely illusory books, but we can do the divine job by self-persuasion and self-convincing. We will never achieve consciousness if we are pleased with our ignorance, lack of faith, and feeble nature.

God is merciful, and the Creator understands that in this material world, in this illusory world, humankind will develop a different understanding, different cultures to cope with their dilemmas.

Edouard Schuré (1960) said that the "truth is immutable in itself; it alone survives everything, but it changes homes and its forms, and its revelations are intermittent." The Almighty allows the truth to be manifested in many ways, different channels, under other forms. The various conditions of manifestations of the truth never change the truth, the same way that the different races never change the essence of human beings.

Only close-minded people, ignorant people, believe that a race makes humans different or better than other races. A human is a human no matter what race a human belongs to. Truth is always truth, even when expressed in scientific or modern terminology rather than orthodox or archaic language. In short, spiritually close-minded people live in the unconscious state. They are not aware of the truth. Therefore, it will be difficult to enjoy a happy life because they will always be irritated when the truth is not presented in a familiar channel.

When we accept the truth, we will become conscious. We will be automatically on the path to becoming one with the Higher Self, the ultimate goal to the end the human race should be marching toward—the fulfilling of God's plan, not our ten thousand fruitless desires. Can we march to that end only with moral laws?

If we believe that only the presence of higher moral qualifications such as righteousness, benevolence, kindness, idealism, and uplifting of the soul are sufficient to do the work of God, the Universe, to fight against evil in this world, we are greatly mistaken. These qualifications are only prerequisites, conditions to be fulfilled, achievements required by the Higher Self, laws that must be obeyed or followed for the qualification to enter the service of God deliberately with a happy heart.

The observation of reality will give us the proof. Do we not see many righteous, measured, human individuals observing the higher moral laws, suffering in the hands of the wicked, and God does nothing to deliver these people, despite their weeping and praying? Why did God not strike down these people devoid of moral sense, violent, ruthless, arbitrary, unjust people who make those who observe moral laws suffer?

The answer is quite simple. The Higher Self will not waste its strength fighting for the cowards. God, the Universe, is interested in recruiting officers or soldiers who have courage, who are not afraid to fight against the adversary for the mission. The despotic, the violent, the liar, the avarice, the wicked, the evil, the murderers are not afraid to impose themselves in fighting for their master, the Devil. Their master loves when they abuse power to enslave others, inflict terror, so their master gives them more power, more wealth, but no health and serenity, thanks to God. Their vices cause all the forms of diseases that come from their addictions. History, in its most recent pages, shows that everyone who works for the Devil, despite their apparent vertical ascent, will eventually collapse sooner or later. The unforeseen will defeat their prudence, and fatality will ruin their plans for the future if they do not put a brake on their demoniac passions and return to the camp of the Higher Self. But when officers, the real soldiers of God, of the Universe, who have courage and achieve ascension, their glory and happiness become eternal.

The point here is to make us aware that we need to observe the moral laws, but we need the strength to go against the world's current, to fight with the enemies for our self-development. That is what is called "many are invited, but few are chosen" (Matthew 22:14 NIV). To fulfill God's moral purpose, we should be linked to strength, courage, and a fighting mind, not a coward. When the fighting mind is present in us, and we are not looking for others, a leader in fighting for us, but merely to inspire us, then the Higher Self will be manifested in us, and providence will protect us from evil. We have to pull our act together, be brave, pray for strength, get up and fight. When we abide by morality and pull our actions together to fight on God's side, we become one with all that is, inside and out, high and low. We become one with the Higher Self and indestructible. Because our faith increases day after day naturally, we keep our oath with God because we no longer have superficial faith. Note that only those who develop a shallow trust cannot keep a vow. It is difficult and practically impossible to meet a person with a superficial faith who is sincere because, according to Lao Tzu (Chapter 23), "[i]f sincerity is lacking it is because of superficial faith." So, such individuals are more likely to be vehicles for prejudices and lies.

Adherence to moral laws is not enough. It is necessary but not sufficient. What we should never forget is that superior morality is a condition to be a cadre for God's government. At the same time, immorality is a condition to be on the crew in evil's government. The choice is in our hands, and we have the free agency to go to any of the two camps. It seems very difficult for an aspirant to make it in God's command, and very easy for an aspirant to make it in the other camp, but do not be a fool, the requirement is challenging for the office of light. Still, the glory is sweet, while the inevitable fall is bitter in the other camp.

Only those who develop consciousness will understand the purpose of moral laws. Morals are the right attitude based upon the proper understandings and proper reasoning. Morals are not based on anyone's dicta, conviction, or opinion. The natural yearning of our pure heart is our penchant toward morality. This yearning inspires us to be determined to take only the proper action to realize ourselves.

God endowed us with the seven principles for self-realization, but not to consume to meet only our physical needs. Only those of us who do not understand the purpose of life live to meet their physical needs; they have no ultimate task of self-realization. We do not have only the laws of the body; we have the physical and moral orders to obey. The rules of the physical body cannot be applied for the spiritual and vice versa because they are opposed, and this opposition weighs on our effort for progress. So, why didn't God create us to face only the moral mandate to quickly achieve our progression in this world? Would it have been easier for us to meet only the moral laws in this world? No, it would have been more painful for us because only our psyche would have taken the shock of moral punishment. The whole world would have been crazier and crueler. In addition, evil people would have more power to abuse the weak people in their minds because the mischievous people would have left less visible evidence of their atrocities on others. The human solidarity for life would have been useless to take it further. The natural physical laws compel us to observe moral laws to have a healthy society. The moral order would have never worked or been possible without the material demand.

Without a community, morality cannot exist, and an organization cannot live without morality. A society cannot exist without morality, justice, and charity because there could not be solidarity without these concepts—solidarity through righteousness, justice, compassion, love, and charity. These concepts are for society, the conditions of all progress, and material prosperity to make people happy through their passage in this world.

The moral is the thin line between inhumanity and humanity. Morals can become so weak in human society that most citizens cannot see there is a crisis. We may have degrees and have a high-paying job, but if we lack moral awareness, we are merely a monster, a dangerous creature for the progress of humanity. History has witnessed that society has experience with many of these types of beings whose purpose in this life was to devour the rest of the world to satisfy their vile desires. These people had faith and took pride in their vicious conduct because they genuinly thought they were doing what was right. Their cruel behavior makes them feel they have power, but history shows that their lives end sadly. We are free to cross the line at any point in our life to be metamorphosized into a savage and degrade the seven principles that make our composition, but not free to choose the consequences as previously discussed.

History also testifies that virtuous people's lives might end sadly too. For instance, when moral people are afraid to shock their fellows through nobly singular conduct, at the end of the day, their life might turn out to be worthless and end sadly with a lot of regrets. There is no need to give examples here because all of us may see or sooner or later meet such people at some point in our lives.

With awareness, repentance, and noble courage, we could cross the line to be transformed into a human being if we were on the inhuman side. We must continuously educate and remind ourselves about the benefits of morals in life and keep the body worthy of self-realization. The equation of life and civilized society will never be balanced without genuine moral value.

Nevertheless, moral laws are what bind. Moral law implies the idea of a link, which is the rule and the measurement of specific facts or certain acts. Generally, the law is defined as the expression of order, the general and constant order by which actions are carried out for good, particularly the law of God and a human-made one that encourages altruism and tolerance. Facts or acts are composed of things, and things have nature, and their life has connections that are imminent. In Montesquieu's (1896) words, the laws are necessary relationships that derive from the heart of things. Indeed, the laws are essential connections that derive from the nature of the circumstances, people's life and actions. There are good reasons for laws because our progression (happiness) in this world depends on adherence to the laws. The teaching of Buddhism suggests that moral laws exist to encourage conduct that embraces a commitment to harmony and self-restraint with the motivation to be nonviolent or free from causing harm (see Thera, *The Buddha's Path to Deliverance*, 1959).

First, we need to develop that internal awareness and intentional ethical behavior, according to our commitment to the path of liberation, to build mindfulness and find happiness in this world. Second, we need to develop that ethical compass within ourselves and manifest it in our relationships with others. Such a task requires us to be voluntarily self-committed to the Higher Self. It mandates creating the sense of self obligation to sacrifice our lower desires, not satisfy them.

If the heart is not pure, we won't develop fundamental knowledge. Suppose we don't have absolute knowledge, which is not conditioned by bias or relative to any emotion or opinion. In that case, we won't build mindfulness, which means practicing mindfulness won't lead to happiness without morals. Let's say, for instance, to illustrate that point, we keep eating junk food every day, and we go to the gym or for a walk a couple of times a week. We try to be aware of what being healthy means. But going to the gym or walking is just a ritual that will not offset the harm of eating junk food every day because we violate the moral code of eating well that goes hand in hand with exercising to be healthy. Practicing rituals will get us nowhere. If we do many stupid, evil things, commit sins six days a week, and go to church the seventh day as a ritual, expecting that we can get rid of our wrong actions and be happy, we are greatly mistaken. And yet this is the principle by which Christianity operated for hundreds of years in Europe before the Reformation. Going to church every Sunday or Saturday or confessing our sins to a priest every week is just a ritual, and no practice will give us inner happiness, but the observance of the matter of the moral law.

If we have good judgment, we should abide by the laws of God and nature and beware of colliding with human justice. Be true to ourselves and be what our destiny wants us to be, not what others want us to be. Therefore, every action in our life should be a step toward our self-development in the right direction, to become divine, and to use the laws as our guide. Note that it is not what we were that counts, but what we are now and will become. Therefore, we must be resolute to be transformed or metamorphosized into divine or luminous beings and die in beauty, very happy.

According to Annie Besant (1947), "we are living in a realm of law, that we are surrounded by laws that we cannot break, [...]." She believes that, "the universe is the emanation of the One, and what we call Law is but the expression of the Divine Nature." The divine nature is impartial. There will be consequences sooner or later when we violate laws, whether natural, spiritual, moral, intellectual, or physical. Hence, sufferings. But if we use the knowledge developed in our lives to conquer the "divine nature by obedience" (in Besant's expression), that is to say, not working against its laws, but with them, we will find happiness here in this world. The divine laws are an absolute necessity in our life. Absolute necessity accommodates God first, then everything that flows from the essence of things. Human laws are a relative necessity in our life. Relative necessity is all that automatically arises from a given condition. This necessity is speculative, conditional. For instance, human laws can be characterized in this category of necessity. The culture, relationships between beings may be used as antecedents to create such laws. Human laws are not immutable, but some of them are necessary. As mentioned previously in the text, we should beware of colliding with human justice to sustain happiness. Because we are constantly interacting with others and having a family, it is very challenging to escape colliding with human justice. But, anyway, we should try to do our best.

Under natural laws, our pursuit of happiness depends on a wide range of conditioning factors and our actions or responsibilities for that quest. For instance, positive consequences will follow if we think or act positively given a set of circumstances, likewise, adverse effects will follow if we think or act negatively.

The physical world is the world of fatality, natural law is the general and constant order according to which facts are subject. For instance, if placed in a particular adverse condition, we have only two necessary likelihoods: a need for action or inaction is imposed on us. Acting here means to react positively, and inactivity, or lack of courage, are considered negative responses. A sudden and fatal necessity is a question of natural law. Placed in such conditions necessarily require our responsibility to act judiciously. While under ethical laws, our pursuit of happiness depends on our full responsibility only. In other words, it depends on our will, desires, the set of our inclinations, or our character.

Whether it is God's, human government's, or nature's laws, consequences will follow to disturb our happiness if we break them.

Chapter 14

Keep the Will Sound and Firm Amid Darkness to Stay Luminous

Darkness occupies more space than light in the universe. So, naturally, darkness tirelessly strives to overwhelm the light, which uses a lot of energy to say luminous amid the darkness. So, if we decide to play the role of light in this world, we must keep our will firm, committed to staying luminous all the time like a star. It is an enormous challenge to be a light in this world, a vehicle for the truth, the agent for the progress of humanity because the evil, the lie of this world, is immense. It is everywhere. Evil is saturating this world. Even though we might be well connected to the Source, the Higher Self, because of our divine purpose, sometimes we may feel engulfed by darkness, evil, and be running out of energy, making it difficult for us to stay luminous. The solution is to keep our faith up because the darkness has no power over light even though evil is soaking this world, making it an incendiary world. It can be powerful only in the absence of light, so strive to say luminous. Darkness is a synonym of the lie, confusion. So, it has no real influence because the light is the synonym of truth, which has tremendous power. The light can dismantle darkness in the blink of an eye. So, strive to keep up the will to stay strong, righteous in the space darkness occupies.

The will is the fundamental source of our acts. God, the Almighty, is the absolute being. We are a relative being, the synthesis of the manifestations of life called to rise and be radiant by an eternal expansion, in the concentric spheres of the Absolute—ascension and luminosity, which depend on our will in Thoth's terms (see Star, 1888). An enlightened will is crucial for us to rise, to say luminous.

Enlightenment should come from transcendental knowledge, wisdom, and God's grace to bend our will in the right direction for our expansion in the spheres of the absolute as a soul. It is essential to rely on transcendental knowledge to strengthen our moral values and will. We must strive to combine divine will, wisdom, and morality to form an existence's precise point. From that point and with a divine straight line for radius, the circle of happiness can be drawn on our life's plane. Any endeavor we are sketching off that intersection with a different radius will create only misery and suffering in our lives. In a word, we will draw a circle outside of happiness.

An unwavering goodwill and faith in ourselves, guided by reason and the love of justice, will lead us to the goal and will keep us luminous amid the vast darkness of this world. Make our genuine will the eyes of our mind, our intelligence. Observe nature at work, germination of acts which proceed from the will, slowly and indeed what the will commands nature to accomplish always manifest.

Remember that our will is a powerful tool we have because, according to Thoth (see Star, 1888) "it is through the will that the Intelligence sees the phases of life unfold." Therefore, if our will is pure, our perception about moral values is set proper, correct, and health, prosperity, and serenity will automatically flourish throughout our life. What a wonderful feeling when we feel wholesome, unsullied, prosperous, and serene! What a wonderful feeling when we strive to create a concordant environment!

One of the sources of the darkness in this world is the myriad of personal and group desires. Both good and evil people want to feel happy. The dilemma is that most of us in this world have a thousand, a myriad of personal desires we wish to satisfy to find and sustain personal happiness. Each individual in this world has a myriad of conflicting desires that contradict each other's individual wishes in this world. In addition, each group or ethnic group has many contradictory desires it wants to satisfy, contradictory to each different group's wishes.

This situation makes it very difficult, even impossible, to sustain happiness collectively in this world because the universe cannot harmoniously help fulfill all of these thousands of desires. So, individuals are fighting with other individuals and groups, nations are fighting to satisfy their desires.

The world has many desires it wants to satisfy, but God has only one plan for this world: unity that can only be achieved by sacrificing personal desires. But, unfortunately, because of the reluctance of the world to surrender its thousand, the myriad of selfish desires, it is experiencing miseries and wars, which seem to have no end.

We want to fulfill our thousand material purposes, but we should be aware that, according to a Chinese proverb, "[d]eath comes one morning, and [our] ten thousand [objectives will] wait." Therefore, there is no way we can satisfy all of our silly desires in this life span. And if we refuse to understand that, we will never be happy, hence incapable of sharing immortality. According to Plato (Timaeus, C. 360 BC, vol. 3, p. 513), "[w]hen [we are] always occupied with the cravings of desire and ambition, and [are] eagerly striving to satisfy them, all [our] thoughts must be mortal, and, as far as it is possible altogether to become such, [we] must be mortal every whit, because [we have] cherished [our] mortal part. But [we] who [have] been earnest in the love of knowledge and of true wisdom, and [have] exercised [our] intellect more than any other part of [ourselves], must have thoughts immortal and divine, if [we] attain truth, and in so far as human nature is capable of sharing in immortality, [we] must be altogether immortal; and since [we are] ever cherishing the divine power, and have the divinity within [ourselves] in perfect order, [we] will be perfectly happy."

To sustain the thrill Plato mentioned, we must make the idea of achieving unity in harmony with God our main task. It is vital to attain unity in God because when we accomplish this task, God will descend into our consciousness, and we can participate in the universe's power. Therefore, make our will the stone of the hearth, the altar of good, the throne of God to enjoy happiness. For God is the indivisible substance, meaning that only in uniting with Him can we achieve self-realization.

It is in our reach to achieve unity with God because we are beings of original spiritual purity connected with the realms of matter in this world. But, on the other hand, the link with the physical makes us destined to go through karmic growth to reunite with God.

According to various religions and philosophies, we were Spirit before being born. This is because our soul was one with God. Our soul is the everlasting part of us. Therefore, when we were one with the Creator before we were born into this world, our Spirit was untouched by gross elements of matter. Therefore, our thinking, emotions, impulses, desires, and aspirations, considered in their energetic aspect, were God's energy because we were one with God.

When we come into this material plane of existence, the illusory aggregate of veils surrounding our fundamental essence urges us to develop our lower ego. The lower ego, the personality, is the veil, the mask composed of various sheaths of consciousness through which our individuality acts. So, we become bound with the material; we become tied with Karma, and we must find our way to evolve through that. The only way to grow is to strive to free ourselves from the hostile powers of this world by self-realization. But remember that self-realization requires a great deal of adherence to moral laws, discipline, concentration, and self-sacrifice.

The influences of the energies or the power of matter on us impel us but do not compel us to develop "desire-body," such as various desires, affections, hates, loves; in other words, the different contaminated mental and physical energies. But despite all the dirty mental powers accumulated, our Spirit retains its quality and essence throughout its entire manifestation into various planes so that we can go through our karmic evolution.

It is the law of God that the heterogeneous matter, the ever-living cosmic Producer, associate, accordingly, consequences to our desires, thinking, and acts sooner or later. Our desires, thinking, and acts have the power to impact our surroundings and rebound. They are the expenditure of energy; that is why we need to do our best to focus on the positives to avoid the negatives manifesting in spades in our life. Remember that we are induced to act evilly, and if we do, we do so of our own volition. We are not compelled, and we have a choice; we are not being coerced to do evil. That is why the universe won't be easy on us regarding the consequences of our evil actions.

To progress within the chain of causation, stretching back into the infinity of the past and the future, we must sacrifice our desires, negative thoughts, and actions. This cause-and-effect of nature's law is known to all religions and philosophies. This law is there to deter us from making adverse decisions and encourage us to focus on positive actions for our evolution.

We may not be aware of it, but we have experienced or witnessed the law of Karma, nature's operation, in action in our life. Ignorance blinded us to see that it was or is Karma in action. When the consequences of our activities turn bitter, we may ask, "why?" And we look for anything to comfort us. We must understand that no fantasies will settle our mind when experiencing the effect of negative Karma. Only developing a genuine understanding of how Karma (nature's mechanisms) is working can comfort our mind.

Negative thoughts, evil thoughts are like viruses, they are very contagious and have the power to do colossal destruction. Tossed like pebbles into the world's mind pool, they could cause negative ripples that could impact millions of minds and instigate harmful desires and actions. Moreover, it won't leave once a negative idea enters this world. Instead, it will encourage copycat evil thinking that will spread like wildfires and create divisions between humankind and God, hence, miseries.

One of the keys to going through karmic evolution to unite with God successfully even in this world is to develop a genuine understanding and awareness of how to mingle three "qualities" in the correlations of force and matter (see Purucker, 1972). It is imperative to strive to establish natural intellectual-spiritual-agility to play with them. The first "quality," one of the divisions of nature, is the quality of longing, passion, and activity. Unfortunately, this noble, muscular quality has an evil side. Blended with any negative aspirations, a virulent and wild compound will form, and instead of a beneficial effect, it will inevitably exert an extremely destructive action throughout our life and our environment. On the other hand, the mixture will form a divine constructive life blended with noble goals.

The second is the quality of truth, goodness, reality, and purity. Like the first one, this quality has its evil side. For instance, overly kind, pure, truthful people are more likely to be victims of bad narcissistic people. Remember the expression "nice guys always finish last," meaning that people who love others more than themselves in this competitive world are more likely to be used by unscrupulous folks. It is a sign of weakness and low self-esteem if we love others more than ourselves. One of the greatest commandments of Jesus Christ is to love our neighbors as ourselves. This second commandment does not say more than ourselves. When we love narcissists more than ourselves, we are not truthful, not good to ourselves. We are not living in reality, we are not balanced. We merely love in excess. Remember the anonymous French proverb (1876) that says, "Excess in everything is detrimental." So even being too nice can be detrimental; that is to say, it can cause unhappiness. If we played smart enough to balance the second quality smoothly throughout our karmic evolution, we would be better off.

The third essential attribute of manifested beings and things is the quality of darkness, illusion, ignorance, and another aspect of the third quality involves inactivity, passivity, repose, rest, or inertia, which constitute the positive side of this quality.

Like threads inextricably mingled, these three qualities run all through the fabric of Mother Nature. They are the phases of our intellectual and spiritual activity. Depending on our mental and moral activity orientation, they function closely to develop or atrophy our consciousness. For instance, a strong desire to be true to ourselves will always benefit us. But, at the same time, the languor for developing a narrow mind regarding morals or living in the darkness will alleviate our misery through our karmic evolution. We will experience fewer sufferings when we get rid of the unnecessary ones. Being passive when it comes to developing darkness and active in supporting the truth, without any doubt, is a noble action.

The idea here is that we need to be skilled at living in this world, in any other world, to continue our perpetual progression through Karma. Every day in our life, we take actions, we think, and sooner or later, we will see the result of our thinking, our actions, whether in this life or one of our future lives. If the thoughts and activities are focused on the positive, we will see positive consequences. Otherwise, we will see negative results, Karma; that is the world we live in. We cannot escape our evolution through Karma, and there is no other way out. Understanding this divine process is the first step toward comforting our mind and carving our destiny. With clean thinking and good actions every day, we can make our future bright and free ourselves from this material world's bondage, or Karma; we can deform it with dirty thinking and actions every day. Why can't we be a co-worker with the Creator? Why can't we put ourselves in unison or harmony with God to develop ourselves, to think like a god? Didn't Jesus Christ urge, according to Matthew (5:48): "Be perfect, therefore, as our heavenly Father is perfect." If humankind couldn't think and act perfectly, Jesus Christ would have never preached to be perfect as the heavenly Father. Note that perfection here means unity with God.

Chapter 15

Learn How to Protect and Use Our Imagination

Some of us may suffer from imagination because of anxiety, depression, delusions, or psychosis. Any imagination related to these problems may be a matter of biology, brain formation, or chemical imbalance. However, this chapter's conversation is not going toward mental illness. Instead, here the conversation about imagination deals with nuisances such as negative fellows working to influence it knowingly or unknowingly, either to take advantage of us or destroy us. Also, the argument is about overcoming negative tendencies when facing situations within our power to change them with our will and the role of imagination in our lives.

Imagination is the image-making activity of the mind; it is the act of creating or reproducing an object ideally not previously perceived. As one of the powerful human faculties, it is the breeding ground for all conscious acts of creation. Despite its fantastic advantages, it also has destructive power. It can make us valuable, good citizen or coward. Positively, the imagination is a rich and fertile ground for creating what we wish to see in our sense of material reality. Unfortunately, evil people can hack our imagination to make us construct false images and fantasize bad things to destroy our lives as well as those of our loved ones. For instance, negative fellows can influence our imagination to make us think we will be better off if we act unwisely. Most of the time, tricky evil people sprinkle their diabolical suggestions with sugar. They use their intelligence to plant negativity in our mind delicately.

Knowing how to protect and use our imagination to make sense of life no matter what happens to us is essential to finding happiness. Regulated by the intuitive and reasoning faculties, our imagination can make us healthy, prosperous, and serene. When the intuitive and reasoning faculties support our imagination and a pure heart bolster it, we have the power to accomplish miracles. For instance, when high morality back-up our imagination, the mind may be balanced automatically, and we will be capable of enjoying great peace. Happiness will flourish like beautiful rose bushes, even though the thorns are there. By the way, life is like bushes of roses that we love to enjoy and our enlightening imaginations may protect us from getting jabbed by its thorns. If we let our unenlightened imagination run wild, we will be getting jabbed always by the sharpest thorns on the bushes of life, and instead of enjoying life, it will be a nightmare for us.

When our imagination is animated by morality, law, and order, our family, the country, the nation prosper. Our life is the manifestation of our imagination; our family's life is our family's imagination; an ethnic group's life is the manifestation of the ethnic group's collective imagination. For instance, in family life, our imagination animates our sensitivity, puts us in a sympathetic mood much more often to live with the temporary absence of a family member, and excites our pity for others' sufferings. Our imagination makes us enjoy the pleasure of family life more actively as well as our freedom. On the other hand, negative imagination can make our family's life bored and unhappy.

It depends on our inclination, and our imagination could be wed with truth or lie. If it is joined with lies, our imagination weakens, and it may go astray without understanding and becomes our guide in domestic, civic, political, and social life. It can direct us to be unfaithful, antipatriotic, the enemy of the law, intolerant, agitator, unjust, irresponsible, and immoral; the path to be an agent of destruction and unhappiness. We will live perpetually in disagreement with the reality of life and the ideal truth if our imagination is not guided by common sense. Without such guidance, our imagination will exaggerate and falsify reality for selfish purposes, make ourselves and others suffer from imaginary events, and even improbable ones, as much as if they were real.

Sometimes our imagination can make us believe that a very dark future is imminent, whereas it is not probable at all. For instance, most of us may have sleepless nights worrying about a job interview, a speech that we have to give for an important event, doing a concert, a review from our supervisors, and all turns out absolutely well. Note that when we let our imagination overrate the harshness of a situation, or people keep telling us that we will fail, we may crash despite our strength to succeed in our endeavors. That is why we need to only let people with positive minds be around us to support us. When we have been confronted with challenging situations, we do not need people who will stimulate our brain to go into overdrive thinking about all the different negative outcomes that could happen. In all fairness, we need true relatives and friends that will stimulate our imagination to solve the problems.

Our negative imagination can thwart our character and make us worried, touchy, gloomy, dreamy, inconstant, jealous, and as a result, we may be fidgeting instead of acting. A sinister imagination has the power to spoil our happiness, in that it could suggest to us to believe that we will never be happy where we are, except where we are not.

Our imagination may make us value something that is not valuable, in mathematic terms, with negative values, under the influence of lust, greed, fear, or ignorance. For instance, our ignorance may make us fall for a person who looks like an angel based on the angelic appearance of that person. So, it may attach all the positive values to someone who may not be valuable or material in an excellent relationship. As a result, we ended up getting trapped and getting down in a lousy relationship later.

Life gives us so many possibilities to be happy, to build happiness. But still, our gruesome imagination may make us believe that we can be more satisfied than others because we imagine that others are happier than they are. We want to be more comfortable than others, and the irony is that we are unwilling to make a personal effort to be satisfied, so we believe that we can steal others' happiness. For instance, we want to leave a spouse, girlfriend, or boyfriend to be with other people's partners who seem to have a happy relationship. Most of the time, when we succeed in gratifying such ill desire, to our disappointment, we find out that we only steal their miseries.

Through our imagination, bullies and haters may try breaking up our relationship with our family to make us and our family miserable. Through our imagination, gold diggers and users make us fall in love with them, or fall for their schemes.

Our imagination can transform us into unconstructive beings who feed on illusions instead of facing our duties and the realities of life. It can disturb our heart, excite our passions, often present evil under the most attractive outlines, and lead us to imminent destruction.

We can never be disengaged from our imagination, which is almost always tricky. Our imagination is like a river that will always flow as much as we are alive. The only attempt to be free from our repugnant imagination is to dry it up, but it is not a river. It is like a river. It cannot dry up. So, we have to deal with it to make sense of our lives and be happy. But, first, we need to be constantly aware of it and know when it is crystal clear or dirty. Once we know it is clear, we can use it, but if it is dirty, we go to the source, the Higher Self, and purify it with the tools God, the Universe, gives us, such as our reasoning, our common sense.

When imagination is united with passions, as a result, we could have a fortunate or unfortunate marriage. Our imaginations can act on our emotions, putting before our eyes—spontaneously, influenced by the will—the image of the object loved or hated, and amplified from our particular point of view. The point here is to develop an awareness of how our imagination operates, how it is influenced, and the principles that govern us, and to understand the actions we can take to entertain a less dark imagination to find happiness.

Remember that we are like a river, which cannot flow without water. Therefore, we cannot flow without imagination. Like a beautiful river in an environment free from pollution, our imagination must be running with crystal clear water. To be healthy, prosperous, and content, we must be running on crystal clear images. Our imagination will not be crystal clear all of the time. A river cannot be clear all the time because bad weather is inevitable. Like nature, which has the power to change dirty water back into a clear one after a storm, we also can turn our negative imaginings into good ones after a bad time. Our imagination can look at any circumstance and change it with brilliant or dark color; it can exaggerate the pleasure hoped for or the pain dreaded in its possession by increasing the attraction or repulsion an event inspires in us. So, our imagination can create positive perceptions or negative perceptions. Positive perception makes us prosper and happy, and negative perception makes us sad and destroys us. All great religions and wise beings warn against any form of anger because, in anger, the imagination grows larger in addition to the reasons that gave birth to it, removes images that could calm it, and only presents those that feed and excite it.

A well-directed imagination is a sure insurance policy for prosperity, health, and happiness. Such an insurance policy, when continuously renewed, increases the joys of the past, erases the sorrows of the present hour, or reassures us with the prospect of a better future. Our imagination can give us hope, animate us, and make us rejoice. But, on the other hand, its illusions may fool us, enchant us, and drive us instead into bitter disappointments. It can embellish the humblest details of life, hide from us, alleviate the shortcomings of those we love, and highlight their qualities; it can dispose us to indulgence and optimism, thus helping to maintain peace in society.

An imagination that only sees the negative side of this life will inspire in us disgust, boredom, and despair. A bad imagination will inspire us to be pessimistic, jealous, and unjust towards those with whom we live. By veiling their qualities and exaggerating their faults, it leads individuals and peoples into social and political crises, making them despise the present for a toxic future.

We cannot afford to be among those with pitiable imaginations who are incapable of seeing the thin red line between right actions and wrong actions. Once we cross that line to go to the wrong side, we open our life to regret, sorrow, misery, and confusion.

Many internal and external factors may affect our decision to cross the line from the right to wrong action. But, external factors are not so influential in compelling us to cross that line unless we give them the strength. And we have no power to change them. So, it is on our internal ones we should focus our attention and use our will to stay on the right side.

Our imagination is an exceptional faculty that has the power to help us create wonders in our life as well as the world. Imagination makes the world turn and makes it what it is today, regarding all the progress and technology we enjoy. But remember that the imagination can also be a dangerous faculty for coaching the propagation of ignorance in the moral domain to make us act foolishly and be unhappy.

Remember that ignorance does not mean that we are a fool. On the contrary, it means that we lack comprehension; it is a lack of knowledge or information in a domain due to a lack of exposure in that given domain, which may be voluntary or involuntary.

It is essential to give good training to our imagination, and always be aware when evil people are playing with it to plant fears in our mind or to stir our emotions and move us in the wrong direction. Do not let people, circumstances, or events spoil our imagination to become fearful.

Imagination is involved in all manifestations of human activity because of its importance in life. We get attention by captivating imagination. Through it, we can master our passions or let them go wild. It has the power to increase human power and happiness when governed by reason. Without imagination, we cannot make sound judgments. Whatever the advantages of imagination, we must be wary of it because it is the "mistress of error," according to Blaise Pascal (Pensées, 82), as well as the truth. We must be on guard against its deviations when searching for the truth in life's conduct, in the direction of the passions.

The effectiveness of our imagination depends on its close relationship with sound judgment. Judgment must control the imagination because it tends to go astray very often, but at the same time, judgment cannot be sound without the help of the imagination. This interdependence makes it difficult for ordinary mindless mortals to balance their moral life to be happy in this world. Moreover, this interdependence makes it difficult for weak people to psych themselves into the proper frame of mind for healthy, legal pleasures.

In the weak minds, imagination becomes disappointing, mistress of error and falsehood, and deceitful in Blaise Pascal's terms (Pensées, 82). In these people, imagination is not directed by common sense but is in perpetual disagreement with the realities of things and the ideal truth. Consequently, it distorts everything, causes suffering, spoils happiness, disturbs the heart, overexcites low passions, presents evil under the most attractive exterior if the subject who possesses it has great wealth and power, and leads to destruction. Also, imagination has a close relationship with passions. Because of this, goodwill, good judgment, and good sense must constantly regulate it.

The imagination can be a blessing or a curse, depending on how it is used or abused. People can use it to encourage virtue or vice, improve or destroy any aspect of life. In Blaise Pascal's terms, the imagination has the power to enlarge little objects to fill our souls with a fantastic estimate, and, with rash insolence, it can belittle the great to its measure, as when talking of God (Pensées, 84). Today, more than ever, with the development of social media, reasoning leaders must educate people about the role of imagination in the practice of life. So, hopefully, we develop some knowledge about imagination to curb it, stay awake, fight the temptation of evil, and enjoy happiness.

Chapter 16

Practice Thoughts Hygiene to Improve Happiness

We must always be conscious that we are human beings. If we lack such awareness, it will be difficult or practically impossible for us to sustain a positive image to stay happy. We have a continuum consciousness, meaning that we can identify with the lower self, our pettiness, in one extreme, and identify with the Higher Self on the other extreme. Our task is to strive not to identify with the lower self but to be aware of it and always be mindful that we should keep taking steps toward the Higher Self. We will never have the power to do that if our mind is not robust. Therefore, we must practice our thought hygiene regularly. But first, we need to understand that we have a psyche with lower and higher functions. Jung (see Journal psyche, 1994-2018) did an in-depth analysis of the psyche, which he defined as "[...] the totality of all psychic processes, conscious as well as unconscious." Jung said that the psyche is an automated system whose purpose is to balance opposing qualities while constantly striving for growth. Jung called the process individuation (see Journal psyche, 1994-2018), which encompasses the philosophical, mystical, and spiritual-intellectual areas of the human being—the immortal part of us, according to the Theosophists. He defined individuation as the achievement of self-actualization by integrating the conscious and the unconscious.

Since our consciousness is a continuum from the lower extremity to the higher extreme level, and that the task at present is to strive to move toward the higher level, we must always seek and stay conscious of the four chief functions in ourselves. Thus, we must be aware of our thinking or intellect, feeling or emotions, instinctive or all inner work of the body, and moving or all the outer work of the body functions.

Our intellect is the capacity to think through reason, then act. It follows the fulfillment of self-discipline and allows us to more easily maintain control over our life experiences with integrity and clarity. The intellect function is the tool the Creator endows us with to reach unity in our diversified world, to guide and preserve us from the perils of this world and make decisions. Thinking brings objectivity to the decision-making process. It is the principle and the synthesis of individualities. From this tool, we can develop our will, the focus of our acts. The intellect is so essential in this world that Thoth (see Star, 1888) said that "the world's realm belongs to those who possess the sovereignty of the intellect," meaning that such people have control over the material, not the other way around. This function has the power to illuminate the mysteries of life. A sound intellect gives us the advantage to gather data to be adapted to the world in which we live and take advantage of it to progress spiritually. As a supplement to our intuition, one of the intellect's functions is to guide us in our consumer world to focus on the realization of ourselves. Because of our training, we make these following questions our primordial: What can we have? What can we keep? What can we increase? What brand of such a product should we purchase to be dynamic, seductive, comfortable in our skin, happy, fulfilled?" From the day we become aware that we are alive to death, these haunting, obsessive questions underline our motivations at all activity levels.

These questions mentioned above are not decisive for a sound traditional intellect, but what are we? How can we realize ourselves? A sound intellect will inspire us to ask these questions just to become wise, live in total inner freedom and perfect bliss, and become the image of the highest possible realization of human beings.

Let us add that when we orient ourselves in such a direction, it does not mean that we renounce all material things in this world. God created or allowed us to create material things to enjoy, but not to be obsessed about them to neglect our progression. He endowed us with an intellect to balance that. So we should use it for that purpose to be happy.

The intellect of thinking functions lets us place an impression from images, ideas, logic, comparing, confirming, denying, verbally speaking, and conceiving. If it is corrupted, nothing positive will come out of us.

The feelings are also a tool that allows us to make decisions. A conventional definition of feeling is emotion. When we make decisions using our emotions, more likely such choices may be conflicted with the rational ones we would have made using our spiritual-intellect tool. Under the emotional-decision-spell, first, we experience joy, then when the spell fades away, sorrow or regret move in, and maybe fear of destruction of our life depending on the nature of the action. According to Carl Jung (see Journal psyche, 1994-2018), feeling is a rational cognitive process that brings decisions into relative worth in a broader and more profound meaning than the previous use. We can say that it is a subjective decision based on what is more valuable or less valuable for our journey through Karmic evolution. Spiritual feeling brings an awareness of how we will receive the decision. First, we may experience sorrow when making a spiritual-feeling decision, then great joy and bliss with time. Because spiritual-feeling choices require a great deal of sacrifice, we may not be interested in making such decisions because of the pain the atonement may bring. We may be more inclined to use emotions to make decisions in our daily life because of the immediate gratification. Hence, we are slowing down the evolution of ourselves and others by generating more Karma during our journey.

Ouspensky (1974) gave a good description of the other functions. For example, regarding the instinctive functions, he distinguished four different classes:

1. We have all the physiological work of the organism, the inner work, which includes digestion and assimilation of food, breathing, circulation of the blood, the building of new cells, the elimination of waste, and secretion.

2. We have the five senses: sight, hearing, smell, taste, touch, and other senses such as the sense of weight and temperature.

3. We have the physical emotions or sensations, the feeling of pain and pleasure.

4. Last, we have the reflexes and the physical memory such as laughter and yawning, the memory of taste and smell, and pain and joy.

The automatic functions are inherent, meaning that they require no skills or training to use them. But, again, if our intellects or thoughts focus on negativities, the intuitive functions can be affected. Our thoughts can make us suffer from indigestion, difficulty breathing, and poor blood circulation. Furthermore, they can give us a false sense of weight, alter our reflexes, give us a false sense of pleasure, and commit all kinds of atrocities on others in the name of love.

The moving functions are all the external movements such as walking, running, and speaking. They are not inherent, meaning that we have to learn and practice them to use them. Again, it must be understood that the thinking function also plays a significant role in these functions. Our thinking has the power to paralyze our movement when faced with danger. Our thoughts may make us healthy or sick, positive or negative beings.

External and internal factors such as our environment and heredity may influence our functions if we allow them to do so. Besides that, there is a reciprocal action on the psyche and the psyche on functions that predispose us to feel, think, and act in a predetermined way, positive or negative, depending on whether we are educated to practice thought hygiene or not. The psyche reacts to the functions, or acts, and the functions respond to the psyche acts, and so on. Carl Jung (see Journal psyche, 1994-2018) said, "The psyche does not merely react; it gives its specific answer to the influences at work upon it." The functions under the influence of external and internal circumstances do not merely react to the psyche. They respond in their way at the end of the day to flourish ourselves and others or make us and others miserable and destroy us or others.

Knowing how to improve our happiness, practicing thought hygiene, is the first step in the process. In the next level, we must work on persuading and convincing ourselves to practice thought hygiene to stay positive, enjoy simple happiness, and help others to be happy. No school, therapist, church, or master has more power than us to do that job. All we need is to be honest with ourselves.

Chapter 17

Look Up to Write a Story

The Almighty sends us into this world with a blank notebook. Assisted by our parents, teachers, and from experiences, we develop knowledge to write in the notebook when we come to the age to start writing. We may write a history or an inspiring story about our life. Some people may argue that since God can know everything, why did God not guide those who will write history to write a good story instead? According to some modern Christian theologians, God's omniscience is inherent rather than total. God chooses to limit his omniscience to preserve his creatures' free will and dignity. God wants us to be happy, thus allowing us free will to change our predestination (wealth, health, deed, etc.), but not divine decree (date of birth, date of death, family, born country, etc.) according to Islam (see The Coran). Unfortunately, every good policy has its unintended consequences. Under the spell of foolishness, some of us may use our free will to destroy our health and wealth.

Not all of us had a good beginning in life. Maybe during

our adolescence throughout the teenage years, even going through adulthood, we were writing our history of self-destruction actions in the notebook. But we need to be aware that the present is here and the future is not there yet, which means that the present and the future are blank pages. Therefore, we still have the opportunity to write something positive, constructive, to improve life; a good story. Having the courage to use the present to document our good story will automatically make us feel better. The present moment is the plain page in the notebook of our life that is open in front of us to write something that will uplift our spirit. And if we continue in that direction every day, we will continue to feel better and better each following day, month, and year. We will face our destiny in a happy state of mind with curiosity, believing that good experiences await us. Good things are coming our way, even though some events may make things hard for us or weigh on our shoulders. But with a positive state of mind, we know that the bad experience shall pass, and it will make us stronger if we survive it. Therefore, we should strive to summon good, uplifting, enriching experiences in our life to write a good story to inspire others. Whatever the events or the circumstances, it is our duty to bring it to good use. We should never surrender to negativities. Such an attitude will demonstrate that we develop a somewhat profound comprehension to sustain happiness.

Note that, like time is moving forward, each current page of our life notebook is constantly flipping forward. And we cannot flip pages backward to edit them because we have no power over the past. The pages are blank in the present time and the future only. And we cannot keep the pages blank once the day opens it. We have to complete our assignments no matter what. Our destiny forces us to write something every day. Therefore, we should not waste our current page doing nothing because inaction is as bad as doing evil to ourselves. If we do not do anything every day, we automatically write a history of doing nothing with our lives.

We will look like fools if we believe that someone can write our story to make us happy. Therefore, it is up to us to strive and do our best to have a good experience no matter what the day brings to us. When things go not as expected, we should look for causes in ourselves, not others. Indeed, nothing has the power to hurt us unless we allow it. But, unfortunately, most of the time, something heartbreaking happens to us because, for some reason, we let our guard down, we were distracted, and others took advantage of us.

Sooner or later, some of us may become aware of whether we have a history or a story. Our perception may improve because of life's continuous pressure, which makes us tired. Suppose we have a story; we should congratulate ourselves because we are on the path of evolution! If we have a history, it is not too late. So, we should stop creating an account now and start working on our story. It will not be easy for us with all the distractions and confusion in this world. The reality of this world is vague and disconnected, lousy.

Notice that many things this world condemns, and on the other hand, it encourages us to do these things to distract us from creating our story. For instance, this world wants us to be healthy and slim and yet, we are being bombarded every second by commercials that encourage us to eat fatty junk food. Pornographies are besieging us by the media, billboards, TV shows, and movies, while this world wants us not to be a sex offender, a predator. On the one hand, this world wants us to love our neighbors, while on the other hand, it promotes hate. It is encouraging us to be a good spouse, father, or mother, and we are being flooded with messages of infidelity. This world wants us to raise our children right, and they are turning them against us. This world wants us to put in hard work to earn our money, and at the same time, it is promoting corruption. The world wants black people to be proud as black, and at the same time, it is promoting products to bleach their skin. Finally, this world wants us to be fair-minded and promotes unfairness.

The enemy is working very hard and is continually kicking us in our neck to force us to look down to create a history of abuse, infidelity, drinking, dosing, sexual predation, crookedness, etc. The enemy's objective is to impose a fake reality on us to have a sensational history, not an inspiring story. We should not play the enemy's game. We must always strive to look up, even when the enemy continues to kick us in our neck to force us to look down. Do not be afraid to feel the pain. Take comfort in the timeless words of James (1:2-4 NIV) to continue pressing forward. "Consider it pure joy, [...], whenever [...] [facing] trials of many kinds, because [...] [knowing] that the testing of [our] faith produces perseverance. [Therefore], let perseverance finish its work so that [we] may be mature and complete, not lacking anything."

We all must experience pain in life, whether emotional or physical, because constant pleasure dissipates, while pain makes us grow and whole when accepted with resignation. Strive to write a story. Do not be afraid of losing the body, dying, so to speak, because the destruction of the body cannot harm the soul. It is the degradation of the body that can destroy the soul. Do not be afraid of dying. Fear of dying does not work as a strategy to create a story. God's decree is that we must be dissolved in the end. It is the law of Karma, and there is nothing we can do about that.

We should make this Epictetus quote one of our favorite ones in this case: "[We] have to die. If it is now, well then [we] die now; if later, then now [we] will take [our] lunch, since the hour for lunch has arrived – and dying [we] will tend to later" (*Discourses*, Book I, Chapter I). Such attitude clearly shows we can distinguish between things we have control over and something we cannot control and should not worry about. Inspired by this quote, we should push ourselves to work on our story because we have the power to do that. And do not think about death. If we must die now, well, we cannot fight this decree; if later, continue working on our story until the hour arrives and enjoy working on it. Note that the beginning of our story does not need to be flawless. That is to say, it is not required that the beginning of our story be pleasing, but we should ideally do our best to end it well.

We cannot develop such a state of mind in one day. We need to practice a lot of spiritual mind development and acquire transcendental knowledge. Focusing our mind on mundane pleasures will not help us in any way to have such a state of mind; these activities will create our history.

All we need to endure the kicking and continue to look up to create our story is to make the Spirit and the Faith paramount. Note that one of our most powerful enemies can be us, our mind, which could be our worst, most mighty enemy. Our mind is the enemy who will inspire us to make an impaired judgment about circumstances that we may regret making for the rest of our life.

We are free to let our mind create the story we want to live. When we force our mind to develop the proper inspiring habits, our mind can be our best friend. Be patient while working on our story, do not rush it, for according to Epictetus (*Discourses*, Book I, Chapter. XV), "Nothing great is produced suddenly, since not even the grape or the fig is. [...] it requires time: [the grapes or the fig must] first [blossom], [...], then put forth fruit, and then ripen." Striving to create a great story so that we can be proud of ourselves is a great thing, and it cannot materialize suddenly. We need to get the proper knowledge, the good willpower, which is the principle of right action, to help it blossom, then enjoy its sweet fruits.

While writing our story, expect nothing, accept everything, and hope that everything will work out for good because we are doing the right thing, and we must steadily link our hope to faith. When we do a good action and do not see a positive result or people pay us back with ingratitude, disrespect, and insult, there is no reason to get frustrated and get angry. Suppose the purpose of what we did was to encourage and inspire ourselves and others, make others happy, and discover wonders in themselves. In that case, we have no right to get angry when they do not appreciate or understand what we did for them. The problem is not them, but our expectation of paying us with gratitude. Gratitude should not matter, just the good action we did.

We should not waste our time persuading ungrateful people that we are valuable; we are better off letting them believe that we are worthless—we should save our energy. Do a good deed and be happy! Unexpectedly, good things will come into our lives sooner or later, and we will live happily. Sometimes, sooner or later, when the blessings are manifested in our life, we may not see the connection with an action we did in the past because of our spiritual development's weakness, or lack of attentiveness.

We must have faith that God will always reward us for our good deeds somehow. But not according to our expectations; for instance, we may expect money, and instead, we may see an abundance in our health, our serenity permeates our life. So we should not express disappointment as a result but rather show sincere gratitude to God. We should always keep in mind that God knows what is best for our evolution at a particular moment in our lives.

Most of the time, our desires may force us to set up a particular objective rhythm that brings the unacceptable or a crisis in our life. For instance, we may have a desire to have kids, and we go so fast in getting a partner that we did not use our intelligence and intuition to see whether that person will be an excellent supporting parent for our kids. We might have violated a moral law or be influenced by our sensual desires, maybe appearance, looks, or money, and choose such a partner. Then, our wish is satisfied, we have the kids, and our partner lets us down; as a result, our kids turn out to be troubled kids.

Remember, according to the Tibetan tradition of Karma (Mcleod, Newsletter), our actions will grow into the four results, which are full ripening, the result from what happened, the result from what acted, and the environmental consequence. So, the objective rhythm choice we play germinates into something that affects many aspects of our life, and we are experiencing a lot of difficulties, and our life turns out to be a nightmare because our dream is shattered; that is the full ripening. We feel lost, get angry, and become harsh, and our pain, our unhappiness, is growing every hour, every day; that is what happened. Unfortunately, we keep playing the objective rhythm continually in our daily life, hour after hour, day after day, and we get another wrong partner and have more kids. Again, our partner lets us down, and they later become troubled kids; that is what acted. Finally, our kids become gang members with a lengthy rap sheet who terrorize the neighborhood, including our home. The worst-case scenario is our kid could become a serial killer; that is the environmental result.

To better understand the concepts of the objective and subjective rhythm, reflect on the following scenario. For example, imagine our desire to open a vitamin store because we want people to take care of their bodies to live healthily, and at the same time, we want to make money. Although it is an objective act, there is nothing wrong with it. Objective actions are necessary because people must act. It is a natural law. Otherwise, there will be no material progress in this world. The problem is the type of rhythm people add to their objectives. For example, in the case of owning a vitamin store, if we did not make a profit after an extended period as we were expecting, and it seems that we are not going to reach our objective, we decide to sell drugs. We did not appeal to the subjective rhythm to solve our problem instead. Automatically, we add a demoniac rhythm to our objective. Very soon, we will have the full ripening of this action. We will have to compete with other stores that sell drugs in the neighborhood. God forbid our competitors are real hardcore gangsters, so our life turns into an absolute nightmare. Now, what happened is that we feel frustrated, get angry, and to survive, we decided to fight and become a gangster. As a result of our action or what acted, we encourage more people in the neighborhood to become addicted to drugs. The environmental consequence is that more people will become drug addicts, drugged zombies, and assaults, break-ins, and robberies will soar in the area to feed their addictions. A crisis we did not expect when we decided to open a store because we had good intentions. Because we rely on our objective rhythm, and maybe because we did not become aware of the power of the subjective rhythm, we did not think about it to solve our problem. Indeed, it would have been the right decision to use the subjective approach to strengthen our objective, make it divine, and avoid going through the process of bad Karma. But, then, all we had to do was to be patient, and sooner or later, our divine dream would have been realized, or accept the loss, practice resignation, and we will have had a terrific story.

Note that our imagination plays a vital role in choosing between the objective and subjective rhythm to solve a crisis in our life. Troubles will find us if we do not have the vision to see the sequence of the consequences in playing a particular objective rhythm before acting. We will never get out of them because we cannot see the benefits of using the subjective approach to turn into blessings the consequence of our objective rhythm actions.

We should know that some demoniac objective rhythms we may play in our life will not grow into the four results. Instead, we may be dead in the first or the second and maybe the third movement. So, our best action is to overcome the crisis and not waste our time complaining, regretting, or being disheartened. As the poet Vigny (1864) says, "Moaning, crying, pleading, is equally cowardly."

Since it is our objective rhythm that brought the unacceptable into our life, only the emergence of a particular subjective or inner rhythm will allow us to overcome the problem and take advantage of the opportunity it brings to develop ourselves and find happiness.

Since they said God is love, why didn't God stop people from making objective rhythm decisions that get them into crisis? People cannot progress, develop consciousness, without trials. "It is circumstances (difficulties) that show what [we are]. Therefore when a difficulty falls upon [us], remember that God, like a trainer of wrestlers, has matched [us] with a rough [adversary]" (see Epictetus, Book I, XXIV). God does not pet us. Instead, the Almighty gives people free agency to choose their problems. Trials are a necessary step for people to establish themselves, and no one can escape this. That is why God tries us but does not put us in a tragic situation. We create our tragedies. The Almighty does not use His imagination to put us in a bad position. He might put us to the test to build us; we put ourselves in a tragic situation to destroy each other. Consider one of Shakespeare's tragedies, *Romeo and Juliet*. In this play, two powerful families, the Montagues and Capulets, decided to be declared enemies. The Capulets were having a party that a group of masked young Montagues gatecrashed, risking further conflict. The young lovesick Romeo Montague, at first sight, falls in love with Juliet Capulets, who is due to marry her father's choice, Paris.

Juliet married instead Romeo, secretly the next day by the county Parish with the help of her nurse. Juliet's cousin, Tybalt, kills Romeo's friend Mercutio in a street fight that Romeo attempts to halt. Then, Romeo kills Tybalt, for which he is banished. In a desperate attempt to be reunited with her secret husband, Juliet follows the Friar's plot and fakes her death by drinking a potion. The Friar sends a message to Romeo about the plot, which fails to reach him. Instead, he learns that Juliet has died. Believing his secret wife is dead, he takes his life in Juliet's tomb. Juliet wakes to find Romeo's corpse beside her and kills herself. After the young lovers' death, the two families agree to end their feud. They become aware that their hatred caused Romeo and Juliet's death and the deaths of Mercutio, Tybalt, and Paris that Romeo kills also. The Montague and Capulet families promise to build a gold statue of Romeo and Juliet to ensure that they end their age-old vendetta for good.

Romeo and Juliet were not the victims of destiny. God would never plan to end his children's life fatally like that. Nevertheless, the two stumbled into their tragedy. Unfortunately, they made a fatal mistake that resulted in a tragic love story.

The main and the secondary characters in the tragedy want

control over others. When we wish things to be in our power that is not, we will indeed create our disaster. To stop making tragedy, we need to control ourselves, not others, in the play of life.

God's trial is a natural initiation of life. Some people will survive a crisis, and others will succumb. It is the survival of the fittest soul, and this is just tough love. The survival of a soul depends on its genuine intention, purity of the heart. If a soul's purpose, for instance, were to create a story, not a history, God would inspire the soul to overcome any crisis. "The righteous person may have many troubles, but the LORD delivers him[/her] from them all; he protects all his[/her] bones, not one of them will be broken" (Psalm 34:19-20).

If we do not do the necessary to use our subjective rhythm to overcome a crisis, our objective rhythm will continue to create more trouble. And no one can help us, not even God. So, the subjective rhythm is the only channel the Almighty can reach out to help us. But, it will be impossible to overcome our problems when we continue to play the objective rhythm because its tempo has these demoniac nuances: pride, arrogance, false prestige, anger, harshness, and ignorance (Bhagavad-Gita, Chapter 16, 4). But, on the other hand, the subjective rhythm makes it possible to overcome our problems because its tempo has these divine refinements: spiritual knowledge, self-control, simplicity, truthfulness, renunciation, tranquility, and fortitude (Bhagavad-Gita, Chapter 16, 1-3). But, in the objective rhythm approach, the demoniac attributes urge people to satisfy thousands of mundane desires; hence they get under the weight of bondage and have a miserable life. Moreover, they are open to many external suggestions, making them prone to lust, greed, and anger.

When using the subjective rhythm perspective, automatically, we are united with God, focusing on our self-development, giving our mind the privilege to deal with the problem with patience in a peaceful, serene attitude.

No mortals can indeed live without desire because this flame keeps us going. But the inappropriate desires to violate God's decrees, such as getting something that was not destined for us at any price or wanting to get something before the time, will surely put us into bondage and consume us. So reducing our thousand objective cravings to the ultimate subjective one will give us more time to devote to God and relax fully.

According to Epictetus (*The Enchiridion*, XV), we come to life as God's banquet guests. To be pleasing guests and enjoy the party that is called life. One of the wise decisions we should make is to take the things served on our table in moderation so that we will not choke. Second, if the Server (the Lord) passes our table, do not complain because that particular food may not be destined to be set on our table or our food is not yet to come. Do not yearn in desire toward it; instead, wait till it reaches the table if it was destiny to set on it. Our patience will be a mark of worthiness to feast with the Almighty. And if we do not grab the things which are placed before us, but can even forego them when we are full, then we will be worthy to feast with the Almighty and rule our behavior with Him. In the end, we will deservedly become divine (our attitude) and be so recognized.

To enjoy the banquet requires a developed discernment, subjective move. Fortunately, we do not need to be highly educated to build our understanding. All we need is common sense, which has the power to open our minds to see that we must be united around God so that He can guide us in our endeavors. If we choose the absurd objective approach, denying that we need God, good religion, or philosophy to assist us, our ego will suffer greatly. And we may never alleviate our distress and will continue to refuse to sacrifice our lower ego for unity. As a result, we will be lost, searching for happiness, gratifying our vain desires, and living in fear.

To bring happiness to our lives, we do not need a fixed framework, a rigid structure, a cage of more or less reassuring mental categories and psychological equations. It is not helpful to freeze ourselves in exclusive teaching philosophy and beliefs to lessen our sufferings.

Besides our traits or characters that may bring and concretize our misfortunes or fortunes, we see circumstances themselves play a significant role. Thus, we should do our best to modify our main tendencies accordingly to create an inspiring story amid the web of major or minor events built around us. Our task in this world is to discern, but not circumscribe, fortunate or unfortunate circumstances and fate constructed as gifts at some point in our lives. It does not matter if the contributions are tasty or poisonous; we must accept all of them with humility. We should use our intelligence to understand that flavor can arise from poison, like poison can arise from the flavor, too, using the philosophical Asiatic representations (see Aubier, 1982).

We have to adapt ourselves to the circumstances to better take advantage of them, knowing that what a user brings to a gift counts, not the gift itself. Similarity, consider card games, it is not the cards' value that determines the winner, but how we play. One may have a valuable card and lose the game. But, at the same time, someone with a lousy hand may win.

So, see life as a card game. For some of us, sometimes fate may give us good cards, sometimes bad cards; for others, either valuable or worthless cards. But, as Schopenhauer said in his *Parerga and Paralipomena*, "Fate shuffles the cards; and we play." And in order not to lose our heads when our luck fails us and to remain serene, we must not only play by the rules of the game of life but also have courage, patience, and intelligence to turn the situation around in our favor. Always remember that we have no power to get rid of unpleasant circumstances in this world, and we have to play with them. Once we understand that, we will develop the proper attitude to overcome afflictions and suffer the least to continue playing until we have to leave the game table.

To sum up, the inner or subjective rhythm attitude we need to develop is the divine attributes to deal with a crisis generated by the objective rhythm. Developing a domineering attitude from the objective rhythm will never solve our problem. On the contrary, we will cause a vicious circle. Note that individuals may play objective rhythm actions that could get them into a crisis, and a nation could do that too. And any attempt to solve its problems without the subjective rhythm approach will be useless.

We must not avoid complicated crises as they may appear, but do not voluntarily look for them either. According to Bailey (1967) they are, after all, only periods or moments of examination of our strength, purpose, purity, motive, and intention of our soul. They will give us confidence when we overcome them and significantly expand our vision. They will invigorate compassion and understanding in our mind because we will never forget the suffering and inner conflict they stir in our soul. They will purify our heart. So, if overcome with resignation, a crisis will increase the light of our wisdom, and our story will be a blessing for the world.

Chapter 18

In the Two Categories of Fools, Always Strive to Be the Smart One

Consider this monologue from the play *Faust* by Goethe: "I've studied now Philosophy / And Jurisprudence, Medicine,— / And even, alas! Theology,— / From end to end, with labor keen; / And here, poor fool! with all my lore / I stand, no wiser than before:" (1-6).

What can make us no wiser despite our knowledge? These lines, which introduce Goethe's Faust character in the first part of the tragedy, indicate a lack of faith in his science. And if we do not believe in our science, we will look like fools.

The peace of the mind is in science and faith in our knowledge, which constructs certainty. We cannot live with doubts and negations. To be happy, we need a fixed point of support. If we doubt our science, we are no wiser than before, no matter how profound our knowledge. Our happiness lies in faith in God and our science of the mind that supports our belief. Knowledge is necessary but not sufficient. We must believe in our science; otherwise, we are fools who are no wiser than before we developed our understanding. We may still be fools even though we believe in our science. In this case, we will be fools aware of our position in the scale of foolishness.

The Book of Thoth (see Crowley, 1969) distinguishes fools in spiritual and material matters. Suppose we are fools in the former category. In that case, with the support of our awareness, we may be acquainted with some immaterial ideas, and our innocence and naivety might benefit us more than our drawbacks. And we may be motivated to use our pages of life to write meaningful stories. While if we are fools in the latter category, our ignorance may encourage us to be engaged in reckless behavior, and our life will be a history of sadness. We will be transformed into machines that are producing negativities. And the negative things in nature we generate in society, which action is equivalent to polluting a body of water that we need to survive, will contaminate our lives, hence destruction.

Strive to be fools with evolving plans, but not fools with viscous material needs. When we are determined to be the former, our heart and mind will work together for noble causes. Then, naturally, we will develop the power to help others in their progression. We will only desire to upgrade others, not degrade them to make them happy because we know that when we harm others, we also injure ourselves. On the other hand, when we are determined to be the latter, we will become greedy. We will be inclined to commit despicable acts, and sooner or later, no matter our position in society or our wealth, we will be subjected to human justice and have a miserable life. Follow history in case of any doubt about that.

They say practice makes perfect. So, if we keep practicing, for instance, playing the subjective rhythm approach to solve our crisis, we will be adept at it and sustain our happiness. But, still, if we keep practicing playing the objective rhythm perspective, we will get into more crises and have a miserable life. So, we will become skilled in everything we practice in this life, whether good or evil, because practicing means that we have faith in it, and it is where we orient our faith that causes our happiness or our misery.

When we know our way, and we are sure our way is the correct one, the way that God wants us to go to reach him to have an incredible journey and be happy, we should follow it. Do not let anyone deter us or lead us astray; otherwise, we will miss our destiny or waste our trip.

Reflect on the following illustration to establish our determination always to follow the path we know for sure. Suppose we have a specific route we take every morning to work, which works perfectly for us. As a result, we always arrive at work at least twenty minutes before the time, and when traffic is heavy, we arrive at work on time. So, one morning because we have an important meeting with some executives to get a promotion, we leave at our usual time, but to get to work quicker, we decide to use our GPS. So, following our GPS takes us to a route with a lot of traffic and red lights.

Consequently, we arrive at work twenty minutes late. As a result, we missed our interview and did not get the promotion. However, if we had followed the usual way we know very well by experience, we would have gotten there on time. The lesson from this story is never to let technology, the so-called experts, or authorities make us change our mind about personal procedures that consistently work for us. If a process works for us, stick to it no matter what.

Merely writing our story is not enough; we need to live it thoroughly while reporting it and continue to live through the content of the inspiring chapters. This approach will make us fully appreciate and internalize our story and enjoy it, and hopefully, others may enjoy it too.

References

Antoninus, Marcus Aurelius. *The Meditations of Marcus Aurelius Antonimus*. Translated by A. S. L. Farquharson. Oxford University Press, 1989.

Aristotle. *Aristotle's Nicomachean Ethics*. Translated by Robert C. Bartlett and Susan D. Collins. The University of Chicago Press, Ltd., London, 2011.

Aubier, Catherine. *Singe*. Avec la Collaboration de Josanne Delangre. M.A. Editions-Paris, 1982.

Augustin, Saint, Bishop of Hippo. *Oeuvres complètes de saint Augustin*. Collection pimslibrary; Toronto. Publisher Bar-le-Duc: L. Guérin, 1864.

Bassi, Ugo. *Ugo Bassi's Sermon in the Hospital*. New York James Pott and Company, 1885.

Basant, Annie. *Karma*. The Theosophical Publishing House, 1947.

Bailes, Frederick W. *Santé Prospérité Sérénité Par La Science De L'esprit*. Traduit par Dr. Noémi Stricker -Rouvé. Paris: Éditions Dangles, 1962.

Bailey, Alice A. *Traité sur les Sept Rayons. Volume II, Psychologie Esoterique*. Editions Lucis, Genève, 1967.

Barbarin, Georges. *Petit Traité Pratique de Mysticisme Expérimental*. Paris: Éditions Niclaus, 1952.

Bhagavad-Gita: As It Is. A. C. Bhaktivedanta Swami Prabhupāda. London: BhaktivedantaBook Trust, 1972.

Blavatsky, Helena Petrovna. *Isis Unveiled: A Master Key to the Mysteries of Ancient and Modern Science and Theology*. Vol. I and II. Theosophical University Press Pasadena, 1988.

Bossuet, Jacques Bénigne. *Oeuvres Complètes de Bossuet*. Besançon: Outhenin-Chalandre fils, 1836.

Bruyère, Jean de la. *Les Caractères*. French and European Publications Inc; Chefs d'oeuvres de l' inconnu édition, 2004.

BMC TEAM. Did Abraham Lie About His Wife Sarai. https://www.pearlofgreatpricecentral.org/ August 2, 2019.

Brady, Adam. How to Use Affirmations to Transform your Life Story. https://chopra.com/articles/how-to-use-affirmations-to-transform-your- life-story/ 2020

Camus, Albert. *Le Mythe de Sisyphe. Essai sur l'absurde*. Jacques Lévesque, "PRÉSENTATIONS." (1985). Les Éditions Gallimard. Paris, 1942.

Chan, Wing-Tsit. *Chu Hsi: Life and Thought*. Chinese University of Hong KONG, T.H.E. 1987.

Descartes, René. *Discourse on Method and Meditations on First Philosophy*. Translated by

Donald A. Cress. Third Edition. Hackett Publishing Company, Inc. Indianapolis, Indiana, 1993.

Crowley, Aleister. *The Book of Thoth (Egyptian Tarot)*. Publisher Samuel Weiser, Inc., 1969.

Epictetus. *The Discourses*. Translated by George Long. Initially Published in 1877. Centaur Edition, 2015.

Epictetus. *The Enchiridion*. Translated by Thomas W. Higginson. Ayra Publishing, Sofia, 1899.

Frankl, Viktor. *Man's Search for Meaning*. Washington Square Press, 1988.

Goethe, Johann Wolfgang von. *Faust*. Translated Into English by Charles T. Brooks. Project Gutenberg Books, 2005.

Goddard, Neville. *Feeling is the Secret*. G. & J. Co., 1944.

Herophilus. *The Art of Medicine in Early Alexandria*. Edition, Translation and Essays. Cambridge University Press, 1989.

Jagot, Paul-Clement. *Traité Méthodique de Magnétisme Personnel*. Éditions Dangles, Paris, 1951.

Jung, Carl. Some Crucial Points in Psychoanalysis, CW 4, par. 665. conscious and the unconscious journalpsyche.org/undestanding-the-human-mind/

Jones, W. T. *Kant and the Nineteenth Century: A History of Western Philosophy*. Harcourt Brace Jovanovich, Inc., 1975.

Latimore, Ed. *Not Caring What Other People Think Is A Superpower: Insights From a Heavyweight Boxer*. Mind and Fist Publishing. First Printing, 2017.

Lucain, Silius Italicus, Claudien. *La Pharsale*. Traduction de Marmontel. Paris. Garnier Freres, Libraires – Editeur.

Lucain, Silius Italicus, Claudien. *Œuvres Complètes*. Avec la Traduction en Français (Classic Reprint) (French Edition) Paperback. Forgotten Books. – December 8, 2017

Mcleod, Ken. Karma As Evolution. Unfettered Mind. https://unfetteredmind.org/karma

Montesquieu, Charles Louis de Secondat, Baron. *Extraits de l'esprit des lois et des oeuvres diverses*. Camille Julian, ed. Paris: Librairie Hachette, 1896.

Mounier, Emmanuel. *Traité du Caractère*. Éditions du Seuil, 1974.

Mencius. *Mencius*. Translated with an Introduction and Notes by D.C. Lau. Penguin Classics, 2004.

Ollé-Làprune, Léon. *La Philosophie Le Temps Présent*. Cinquième Édition. Paris, Berlin Frères, Libraires–Éditeurs. Rue de Yaugirard 52, 1952.

Ollé-Làprune, Léon. *Essai sur la morale d'Aristote*. Paris: E. Bélin, 1881.

Ollé-Làprune, Léon. *De la Certitude morale*. 1 vol. in-8°, Paris, 1880, Belin frères. 5« édition, 1905.

Ouspensky, P.D. *The Psychology of Man Possible Evolution*. Vintage Book Editions, January 1974.

Pascal, Blaise. *Oeuvres Complètes*. Édité par Jacques Chevalier. Bibliothèque De La Pléiade. Librairie Gallimard, 1936.

Pascal, Blaise. *Pascal's Pensées*. Introduction by T.S. Eliot. E.P. Dutton & Co., Inc., New York, 1958.

Purucker, de G. *Occcult Glossary: A Compendium of Oriental and Theosophical Terms*. Theosophical University Press, Pasadena, California, 1972

Plato. *Timaeus*. Translated by Benjamin Jowett. CreateSpace Independent Publishing Platform, 2018.

Saint Thomas. *Oeuvres Complètes*. Project Docteur Angélique. http://docteurangelique.free.fr/fichiers/ListeDesCoursAvecliens.htm.

Sarte, Jean Paul. *Huis clos, suivi de Les Mouches*. (Folio) (French Edition) Pocket Book-January 1, 1972.

Seneca, Lucius Annaeus. *On the Shortness of Life and On the Happy life*. Edited by Stephen Abbott. Abbott ePublishing, Manchester, New Hampshire, 2009

Seneca, Lucius Annaeus. Of Providence. Translated by Aubrey Stewart. Montecristo Publishing LLC, 2020.

Shakespeare, William. *Oeuvres Complètes*. Traduction de Pierre-Jean Jouve et Georges Pitoëff. Bibliothèque De La Pléiade. Librairie Gallimard, 1959.

Schopenhauer, Arthur. *Parerga and Paralipomena: Short Philosophical Essays*. Volume I. Translated and edited by Sabine Roehr, Christopher Janaway. Cambridge University Press, 1957.

Schopenhauer, Arthur. *Parerga et paralipomena: aphorismes sur la sagesse dans la vie*. Traduction Cantacuzène. G. Baillière et Cie, 1897.

Shuré, Édouard. *Les Grands Initiés*. Librairie Académique Perrin Paris, 1960.

Slater, Wallace. *Raja Yoga*. Sixth Quest book edition, 1994.

Star, Ély. *The Mystères de l'Horoscope*. Éditeurs Hector et Henri Durville. Paris, 1888.

Sokoloff, Boris. Predisposition to cancer in the Bonaparte family. M.D.https://www.sciencedirect.com/journal/the-american-journal-of-surgery. Published by Elsevier Inc.,1938.

Thera, Nyanatiloka. *The Buddha's Path to Deliverance*. Pariyatti Press. Buddhist Publication Society, Second Edition, 1959.

The Holy Bible. New International Version. Biblica, 1984.

The Holy Quran (Koran). Translated by Abdullah Yusuf Ali. King Fahd Holy Quran, 1987.

The Tao-Teh-King: Sayings of Lao Tzu. Translated with commentary by C. Spurgeon Medhurst. London: Quest Book, 1975.

The Complete Poetry and Prose of William Blake. Annotations to An Apology for the Bible by R. Watson, Bishop of Landau. Edited by David V. Erdman. London, 1797.

The Jungian Model of the Psyche. Journal Psyche, 1994-2018.

The Jung and his Individuation Process. Journal Psyche, 1994-2018.

Tocqueville, Alexis de. *De la Démocratie en Amérique.* London: Saunders and Otley, 1840.

Thoth. *The Emerald Tablets of Thoth The Atlantean.* Translated by M. Doreal, Illustrated by Kristen A. Vasques. Source Books, Inc., 2006.

Vigny, Alfred de. *Les Destinées: Poèmes Philosophiques.* Michel Lévy frères, Paris, 1864.

Wikipedia - *Reincarnation.* https://en.wikipedia.org/wiki/Reincarnation

Yamamoto, Kat and Lloyd Robert A. Ethical Considerations of Japanese Business Culture. Journal of Business Diversity Vol. 19(2) 2019.

About the Author

Yvon Milien was born in Port-au-Prince, Haiti, and received a degree in civil engineering from the Technical Superior Institute of Haiti. He earned a Bachelor of Science degree in mass communications from the State University of Haiti, where he wrote a thesis, *"Position de la Presse dans la Vie Sociale Haitienne: Recherches sur l'Orientation que Donne le Contenu Educatif de la Presse pour Equilibrer la Vie Sociale"* (The Press's Position in Haitian Social Life: A Study of the Orientation of the Content of the Media to Sustain Haitian Political and Social Life) for the Department of Human Sciences.

In 1997, he obtained a Master of Science degree in sociology from Brigham Young University, where he wrote a thesis titled, "Haitian Mormon Converts Dwelling in New York City: A Cross-Cultural Perspective in Understanding, Interpreting, and Experiencing the Mormon Subculture."

In 2000, he obtained a master's in international relations and a master's in public administration from Syracuse University, where he wrote a thesis paper titled, "Fostering Democracy and Human Rights in Haiti: An Examination of Haitian Democracy."

In 2004, he earned a master's in education from the City University of New York, where he wrote a thesis titled, "The Effectiveness of Graphic Organizers and Baxendells's Guiding Principles for Instructional Practices with Special Needs Students."